Pillars of Fire

This is, **L. Mason Jones**, second book. He served a number of years in the military, and travelling on a so-called 'government service' passport, found himself in such places as south Yemen, Bahrain, the Gulf of Oman, Cyprus and Germany. After leaving the service he became part of the team producing the highly successful business jet, The Hawker 125. He functioned as a quality engineering inspector with, initially, British Aerospace then Corporate Jets Inc and finally Raytheon USA, the latter of which purchased the thriving business and moved production to the USA. Mr Jones then left the business to concentrate on writing projects. He has three adult offspring and resides in Chester.

By the same Author -

Monkey Trial 2000

Pillars of Fire

L. Mason Jones

Arena Books

Copyright © L. Mason Jones 2019

The right of L. Mason Jones to be identified as author of this book has been asserted in accordance with the Copyright, Designs and Patents Act 1988. All characters and events described in this book are fictional and any resemblance to actual persons, living or dead, is purely coincidental.

First published in 2019 by Arena Books

Arena Books
6 Southgate Green
Bury St. Edmunds
IP33 2BL

www.arenabooks.co.uk

Distributed in America by Ingram International, One Ingram Blvd., P.O. Box 3006, La Vergne, TN 37086-1985, USA.

All rights reserved. Except for the quotation of short passages for the purposes of criticism and review, no part of this publication may be reproduced, stored in a retrieval system, or transmitted, in any form or by any means, electronic, mechanical, photocopying, recording or otherwise, without the prior permission of the author or the publisher acting as his agent.

L. Mason Jones
Pillars of Fire

British Library cataloguing in Publication Data. A Catalogue record for this book is available from the British Library.

ISBN-13   978-1-911593-53-9

BIC classifications:- HBG, HRA, HRAC, HBTD, JFCX, HRAX, HPX.

Cover design
By Jason Anscomb

Typeset in
Times New Roman

INTRODUCTION

Poor Ezekiel took a full week to recover; he almost went out of his mind, a *traumatic* event that now would be called an 'encounter of the Third Kind'.

What *was* it the Prophets and Patriarchs saw?

Things that amazed them and filled them with awe?

They looked up in wonder, at the blue sky, saw 'flying shields', 'Moving Stars'. Things that didst fly.

'Angels' descended with news from on high, they rose up again, after counselling men, on 'Pillars of Fire' to the sky.

Rose up to what? We surely must ask. To *Heaven,* they *thought.* But *now we may* think… Perhaps it really was not.

Was it a 'structure' within a thick cloud that once didst come down on Sinai's high ground? With thunder and 'trumpets' and unearthly sound.

Was it all due to an earlier plan? When 'unearthly' beings arrived to 'make' man?

Did they choose an earth creature, a primate perchance? ……

Then cause its small brain to greatly enhance?

A great brain develops in advance of its needs, just to till ground and plant all those seeds.

The Newton's and Einstein's later appeared. These were the 'New Gods' that many revered.

And so this great brain, with is penchant for maths, could study the planets and learn of their paths.

It will not stop there, "With these assets of ours". First to the planets and then….. To the Stars.

CONTENTS

CHAPTER I	ANGELS OR ALIENS?	Page - 5
CHAPTER II	CREATOR OR CREATORS	Page - 16
CHAPTER III	THE 'ANGELS' OF ABRAHAM	Page - 50
CHAPTER IV	THE 'ANGELS' OF EXODUS	Page - 58
CHAPTER V	WEAPONS FROM THE 'ANGELS'	Page - 67
CHAPTER VI	ANGELS OF THE ANCIENT EAST	Page - 75
CHAPTER VII	PILLARS OF FIRE	Page - 94
	CONCLUSION	Page 119
	REFERENCES	Pages 157-162

CHAPTER I

'ANGELS' OR ALIENS?

This work is a close study of the activities and actions of beings the patriarchs terms 'angels', avidly described in the old testament.

The Old Testament contains a statement that makes it abundantly clear that the seed of David would be removed and used to create a special entity later, who was often referred to in the New Testament as 'thou, Son of David', and *that is Jesus himself.* In the book of Samuel in the Old Testament a *telling statement says* [1] 'and when thy days be fulfilled and thou shalt sleep with thy father's (death) I will set up thy seed *after thee which shall proceed out of thy bowels'* (specimen removed after the death of David). This cannot be interpreted in any other way than genetic reproductive material remove, preserved and later utilised to produce another very special entity. To be sure, David's seed produced Solomon, allegedly the wisest of kings who, like his father David, was familiar with, *and* looked after the awesome weapon known as the Ark of the Covenant.

Many cases are highlighted in this work, taken directly from the old testament of the angels carrying out genetic implants to produce their special entities for specific tasks.

Further clear evidence citing David as the 'donor', or supplier, of the genetic material used by the 'angels' to produce their emissary Jesus, is provided in Luke's Story,... [2] "And behold, thou shalt conceive in thy womb and bring forth a son and shalt call his name Jesus. He shall be great and shall be called the son of the highest and the Lord God shall give unto him the throne of *his father David"*.....

To be sure, many people over the centuries have accepted the writing in the Old Testament, regarding the activities of Angels, unquestioningly, and have been happy enough to have accepted them as divine representatives of God. To a serious reader today, their actions, particularly those of the Exodus account, are so incredible that we are almost *compelled* to assume a different interpretation of them. This is easy for current humanity, when we can relate them to our own scientific capability, but in biblical times, this was not possible. Nevertheless, enquiring readers of those times must have been their actions as high profile, warlike behaviour in assisting, directing, encouraging and indeed *drowning and annihilating* an entire army and surely must have struggled to view their activities as divine. Yet, they still seem to have allowed the retention of the image, accepted for centuries, of angels as entities with wings, halo, an innocent expression and long white apparel.

Today, many people, although professing to be confirmed Christians and accepting the validity of biblical writings, suggest that these fantastic accounts of Angels and their questionable activity are not to be taken too seriously. This is not possible, either they are truthful accounts related by the patriarchs of what they actually witnessed, or they are not. If they are not, then how many other accounts in the Bible must come under suspicion?

Even the most atheistic people on Earth would probably agree, that it would be most unwise to disregard the Bible in its entirety as a serious source of data and, most certainly, this view would be supported by the many archaeologists that have been involved in past and present archaeological digs in the middle East.

If we accept that the Patriarchs, such as Abraham and Moses, did actually exist, and that they were truthful, 'God fearing' men and not just imaginative writers and storytellers (or downright liars), then we would also have to accept that their very close encounters with beings that 'descended' and communicated with them in their own language did actually happen. These beings were interpreted by the Patriarchs and other biblical characters, as divine Angels (or messengers) of The Lord. This interpretation has also been accepted by countless people down through the centuries, *and they may be perfectly correct*. However, the cold fact is that many people, after reading the biblical accounts of their interactions with humankind and their questionable activities (who may not be inordinately religious) may, from a few paces back, as it were, put a totally different interpretation on these beings. Abraham and Moses were involved in many alarming and traumatic events with these angels, who very closely involved themselves in the affairs of men in biblical times, yet seem so conspicuous by their absence in modern times.

If these angels were from 'heaven', and of course heaven is, clearly not a place on Earth, then these angels could be interpreted as 'extra terrestrial' or 'off Earth' entities. The pages in the Bible are replete with dramatic activity involving angels. These beings could also be termed angels of death, if the events of the 'Passover and the Hebrews' subsequent battles in the desert are truthful interpretations, simply because the Bible tells us that these 'angels' led, directed and 'went forward' to actually annihilate masses of humanity, and state in Exodus in one case, to slaughter every living creature they encountered. It is entirely logical; therefore, that many people would find it difficult to assign a title to such beings as 'Divine Messengers' of the Lord, whose own commandment is 'thou shall not kill'. The best description the Patriarchs could give with regard to the mode of transport of the 'angels' was a 'cloud They frequently descended on a 'cloud', or a pillar of a cloud. When one observes the almost perfectly formed disc-shaped or so called 'lenticular' clouds that exist in clear weather conditions, the 'angels' form of transport becomes quite interesting, but it seems more likely that water vapour was produced and utilised by these entities to *purposely disguise an alien structured craft.*

Nevertheless, these amazing beings were interpreted by the biblical characters as 'divine angels', who seemed very concerned in assisting Moses and the Hebrew people to achieve their goal of obtaining land (although occupied at the time) that was promised to *them*; and in achieving this aim, misery and death was heaped upon, firstly, the Egyptians, then anyone else who stood in the way of their attainment of their promised land. After the exodus from Egypt, Genesis Book 1 and 2, together with the Exodus account, are descriptively written by Moses detailing the actions of the 'angels', not only with regard to himself, but also to his predecessor, Abraham, when even more dramatic events occur, with angels destroying and annihilating with equal gusto as they were to do during the days of the Hebrews' battle in the desert wilderness. Their actions in assisting Moses and the Hebrews were certainly impressive enough to make Moses take the trouble to avidly record it all.

A few centuries ago, life was fairly straightforward and simple in the Christian world. God-fearing men tilled the ground, observed the Ten Commandments, went to church, then rested on the Sabbath. They went off to war with great pride when the occasion demanded, thought nothing about killing as God was, in any case, on their side. In time they mostly married and, together with their wives, raised families to observe the self same code.

Then along comes the so-called age of enlightenment. Those who were not inordinately religious took it all in their stride and with avid interest. Others, with strong religious leanings, suffered a bit more with a certain amount of cultural shock and social disorientation. Slowly but surely the revelations of science began to erode away at once firm and comfortable beliefs. Earth is not the centre of all creation and was not created in 4004 BC at 09.00am Greenwich Meantime. The Earth travels around the Sun and not the other way around. Those little points of light are other suns, enormously far away. Men began to wilt a little in awe of their own, now apparent insignificance.

While still reeling under the onslaught of these revelations, along comes the 'New Messiah', Charles Darwin, to shake the religious establishment to their foundations and with the added 'trauma' of informing men they were not created by God at all, but descended from monkeys. Many men have longed for the heady days when such people would have been burned at the stake for such pronouncements.

However, the centuries have rolled by since the time when the shocked church elders refused even to look through the eyepiece of Galileo's telescope as he tried to explain the significance of his discoveries to them. He implored them 'At least to look for yourself'.

Gradually, Galileo and many that followed him, slowly but surely, made humanity aware of its precarious and quite unimportant position in, not only our galaxy, but in the entire vast universe. Now, science was calling all the shots. People began to trust in it, wanted to know more. Brilliant people emerged, such as Newton and on down to Einstein and others, probing into the very secrets of life itself. The pace gathered, faster and faster the discoveries rolled in, progress gathering momentum in all quarters.

The equations of Einstein, the study and discovery of smaller and smaller atomic particles, the advances in medicine and genetic science. In a single lifetime people witnessed the first String bag aeroplane lift into the air in 1903 right up to the point of a soft landing on the moon, the greatest leap forward in advancement that any century has witnessed. Now, specially designed cargo aircraft take to the sky that are large enough to have had the first short hop of manned flight taken place *inside* of them. Aeronautical designers now consider one thousand seater passenger aircraft as quite a feasible proposition. Aircraft designers envisage craft rather like the shuttle but with power sources suitable for both space travel and earthly manoeuvres within the atmosphere. However, for all that, it is slowly beginning to dawn on people that for all our advancements, science *doesn't* have all the answers, that people expected rather a *lot* of them. Indeed, in some cases, like the churchmen before them, *they* sometimes refuse even to consider any alternative to *their* established theories, and anything that does not fit in with these assumptions is simply labelled 'unscientific' and may simply remain unclassified and consigned to some dusty museum basement until more enlightened times. In the significant year of 1947 a series of dramatic events shocked the scientific groups, causing almost as much shock as Darwinian revelations did to the religious factions, and science has been reeling under it, and trying to come to terms with it ever since, and that is, of course, the coming of the UFO enigma. Now, we have the strange scientific contradiction put out at the conclusion of the Condon Report, "Further investigation of the phenomena would not advance the cause of science" and, "They are simply natural phenomena our physicists do not yet understand", which says of course, we don't understand it, but further investigation would not help us to understand it!

PILLARS OF FIRE

Books poured off the presses on 'flying saucers' and UFO related events. As these began to get a bit repetitive in mostly trotting out the same cases, data and photographs, more and more way out topics began to be considered. Earth forces, leylines, pyramid power, standing stones, middle Earth dwellers, translunar phenomena, structures and the Moon and so forth. Then, with the advent of the lunar exploration programme with the Mercury, Gemini and Apollo projects, culminating with out 'descending on a pillar of fire' onto another world, we finally begin to ask ourselves, *could this have all be done before?* The UFOs had not gone away, they apparently accompanied all the missions in earthly orbit, and all the flights to the Moon, and were reported in the vicinity of, *and on*, the Moon itself.

We began to ask, where do they go to have their accidents? Surely, they can't stay one hundred percent serviceable all the time? We fill this question gap by stating they have crashed and are, in fact, under wraps in some remote location, being quietly studied. Even alien body forms are being medically studied closely, equally as much as all the victims of the alleged abductions.

The hypnotic experts come on the scene and 'regress' people back to their traumatic abductions. In some cases they almost jump out of the chair in excitement and fear and have to be quickly brought out of their trance. The 'regressers' **still** don't believe it all, stating that the victims simply believe it to be true. Brave new writers and open minded publishers appear, asking was Jesus an astronaut? With no chance of being burned at the stake.

Some almost demanded explanations of legends, edifices, artifacts and anomalies in human history that did not fit in with the established order. On top of this was the burning issue of what was in our skies? That people all over the world were observing, and the more science side-stepped, disregarded and debunked it, the more the momentum gathered among those demanding explanations for this strange phenomenon.

The religious factions were rather bemused by it all. Now it was the turn of science to be 'on the hook' so to speak. They had been at loggerheads with cold, logical science for centuries and an uneasy truce prevailed. A solution to blend to two views together was sought – forget the seven 'days' for the creation of the universe. After all what person has not heard the expression 'things were never like that in my 'day'. A day now became an *era* and not a period of twenty-four hours; and what about the so called 'big bang?' Even science, with all their logic, cannot explain a mass of hydrogen coming into existence from nothing. So, let *this* have been divine creation, the primordial ball of hydrogen the 'egg' of creation exploding violently and massively on divine command, 'Let there be light'.

PILLARS OF FIRE

And so, the delicate impasse prevails and the Christian church survives and seems quite able to argue its case with the scientists. Therefore, the dualistic arguments rumble on and, in certain southern states of America, remain quite heated over ninety years after the Tennessee townsfolk tried to lynch a certain John Scopes, for daring to teach evolutionary concepts with regard to human origins to his class.

Today, however, the argument is now no longer dualistic. Another concept, equally as bold as Charles Darwin's pronouncements, has entered the arena and will emerge within these pages.

Godless eastern European doctrine once stated: 'Religion is the opium of the masses'. In a sense this is true, because religion, blind faith or ardent belief, or whatever we wish to call it, has brought comfort and succour to many people over the ages. It can also be said to have brought death and destruction to many races once existing under their own godless, but nevertheless, workable and functioning existence, and a few examples are the North and South American Indians, not to mention countries invaded by the Crusaders.

Nevertheless, people have used their religious beliefs like a warm coat, tightly wrapped around themselves, indeed, sometimes covering their ears and eyes with it to keep out the cold, advancing logic of science attempting to introduce doubt and troublesome uncertainty into their beliefs.

It would seem a great pity if the admirable doctrines of Christianity are all eventually allowed to dissipate and all the warm coats are discarded forever, as science itself may fail to provide a better garment and is sometimes itself subject to tunnel vision and 'the ostrich syndrome', and a few examples are the many problems that bedevil the accepted Darwinian theory for human origins and the complete refusal to consider aerial phenomena as anything but natural occurrences that our physicists do not yet comprehend, in spite of the sworn testaments of whole armies of competent individuals who have been unfortunate enough to have had an encounter at close quarters with the unexplainable.

However, it would appear that the process of discarding the religious coats has already begun. There was a time when the people who turned up late for the church service had to stand at the back of the church by the draughty entrance door, while the pews creaked and groaned, filled with people of all ages.

Nowadays, the masses appear to be far less inclined not only to stand at the back of the churches, but to even fill the pews, and sadly, in certain areas, the churches even have to lock their doors when no service is taking place in order to prevent the sacrilegious plundering of the collection boxes, now, the last sanctuary of desperate people is being denied to them.

Who or what is to blame for this unfortunate situation? Certainly not the godless doctrines of Eastern Europe, whose system has been tried, tested and found wanting. The blame lies fairly and squarely at the door of science.

It began with the probing telescope of Galileo and his contemporaries and continued on to 'the age of enlightenment', followed by the advent of all the sciences. First the astronomers, then the geologists establishing the true age of the Earth, onward to the archaeologists, paleoanthropologists and finally, the seemingly outrageous atheistic pronouncements of the Darwinian theories firing the broadside into the flagship of the divine creationists, the results of which was the slow, but inexorable sinking ship. However, there were survivors and they now hold tenaciously on to their newly built fortress and are able by bending a little with the wind and modifying their views a little to be seemingly holding their ground, and the battle rages on.

Strangely, many people wrapped up in this dualistic argument, that continues as strongly as ever it did in certain Southern States of America and elsewhere, fail to consider the possibility that we may all be missing the point entirely and that the profound possibility exists that we may eventually have to consider a rather fantastic, but nevertheless possible 'third alternative' for the origin of the human species on Earth.

This view is particularly reinforced by the fact that even theologians now consider certain stern unreserved pronouncements in the Genesis account of human creation, as standing little chance of surviving logical analysis. But the so-called 'evolutionists' have also struggled and failed for over a hundred and fifty years to prove their case, and the vital fossil links still evade them. Consequently, the aim of this work, therefore, is to look at the so-called 'third alternative' but, in doing so, to be in no way derisory or blasphemous of the established and respected religious writings, but simply to reflect on the biblical accounts of these strange happenings involving 'angels' and to stand back a little and 'have another look', so to speak.

This prospect is something that would have been unthinkable a few centuries ago, unless one had a 'death wish' in spite of imaginative writers and theorists, such as Cyrano-de-Bergerac and Leonardo Da Vinci. It may have even been unthinkable before the advent of rocketry, followed by manned excursions and lunar landing objectives. But more importantly, a significant theory that jolted us all out of our aforesaid dualistic viewpoint on the still unresolved question of human origins, is, the profound possibility of an extra-terrestrial intelligence having been involved and seemingly still involved in human affairs. This is not so much due to Kenneth Arnold, with his 1947 encounter, but the sensational dailies, who misquoted him and coined the phrase, 'flying saucer' followed by questions such as 'Who are they? What do they want? How long have they been here? What are they to do with us? What will be the culmination of it all? Why do 'they' appear to be removing so many people from the Earth to extract genetic material, are they the descendants of the same entities that roared and boomed on the mountain tops and moved on 'pillars of fire', now so further advanced that they can dematerialise before your eyes, or from the radar screens of intercepting craft? Why this enormous interest in humanity? What is it all about?

The first chapters of this work will deal primarily with the interesting events and encounters with angels against the backdrop of our modern day technology. There is an amazing amount of them, and to deal with them all would require a Volume II. When looking at them from a few paces back, in what could be termed as a cold, scientific manner, it becomes apparent that they could be viewed as being open to quite a different interpretation than that intended by the biblical writers and, even if we do accept the existence of the biblical Patriarchs and their stories of angels, but assume that those amazing events were all fabrications with good intent, that is to help reinforce and have accepted the religious doctrines, we still have to ask, where did the inspiration come from, and what may they have seen in order to be so descriptive of aerial phenomena that we can identify with them in terms of modern day reports almost as though it was the same phenomena?

If accepting the existence of the Patriarchs and the accuracy of their writings, then the further we get into the reports of their encounters with their angels, the more we feel that we could easily substitute the word 'alien' for angel. Therefore, if the accounts in the Bible, seemingly involving off-Earth entities (remembering that this description applied to both divine angels and aliens) are not simply the aforesaid embellishments of earlier Sumerian or Babylonian legends or dramatic renderings from the fertile imaginations or literary talents of Moses and others, then we have to assume that at least some of the accounts that impressed the biblical characters so much for them to write so descriptively about them, were real, or at least based on real occurrences, and this, clearly is very profound.

It must be true that the world as the ancients knew it, was a large and impressive place, when every journey had to be made, for the most part, on foot, or camel and as for the shrinking world that we are aware of today, their world was largely unexplored and lay firmly under their feet as the centre of creation, with the heavens above and the Sun dutifully circling it.

PILLARS OF FIRE

The ancients had no conception of the twinkling stars being other suns with the possibility of attendant planetary bodies circling them and perhaps having multi-cellular, reproducing, maybe even intelligent life forms upon them. Thoughts of off-Earth intelligence existing probably never entered their minds and to them, 'up there' meant heaven rather than interstellar space. Therefore, as a consequence, if the angels were in fact aliens, they could masquerade as the former to their heart's content and be accepted by the witnesses of the encounters as exactly that.

Therefore, to the ancients, impressive beings 'coming down' on 'pillars of fire', on in the form of a 'cloud', and so forth, were simply interpreted as angels of the divine creator coming among humanity to control the privileged chosen ones (or possibly, created 'hybrids') on Earth to do their bidding, or directing them, and other selected or correctly functioning beings, away from the holocausts or wrath of the Lord that was about to descend on the iniquitous cities and the malfunctioning creations contained therein. Nowadays, of course, having descended ourselves on other worlds with 'pillars of fire', either manually in the case of the lunar excursions module, or remotely in the landings on Mars and Venus, our science, coupled with our cosmic awareness and advancements, and our postulations on the possible existence of other world intelligences, allow us now to review with renewed interest, just what it was that the ancients may have been witnessing, with all those 'moving stars', 'chariots of fire', 'flying shields', pillars of fire' and booming voices from mountain tops warning the Patriarchs to tell the people to keep clear or die, and so forth.

If we do put an extra terrestrial interpretation on them, this factor could be more than just interesting speculation. It would be quite fantastic, and the natural follow on to this would be to question the whole reason behind such avid interest and deep involvement in the affairs of humanity up to the point of deciding who will live and die and proceeding to go about the process in such a cool, ruthless, determined and detached manner.

Surely, the only answer to such speculation and assumption that the angels are actual beings from another world and not 'heaven', must be to assume that they must have been very involved in the origins of humanity in the first place.

The seemingly science fiction/fantasy viewpoint that humankind may be 'property' made decades ago, that included the profound possibility that the Garden of Eden was an organised and chosen genetic experimental centre, specifically for the production of the human entity from a simian type of ancestor, might just be true. This would certainly account for the unexplained over-endowed and quite awesome human intellect, where the obvious traits are our own superb creativity and the unconscious wish to 'return to the stars' is so evident, and the most unlikely possibility of our intellect being a simian bequest.

As sure as tomorrow, this intellect, however we came by it, will ensure that eventually we will enter deeply into the abode of the creator(s), which may well have been the intention of it all in the first place. It does seem strange that the whole idea, in spite of all our aforementioned cosmic awareness and enlightenment and actual designs of interstellar craft, seems just as preposterous and fantasy-prone as ever, but this seemingly way out assumption would explain a lot of things, including the sheer volume of reports from the angels of Abraham, down through the 'ages and pages' of our written history of aerial phenomena. It would obviously also explain the aforesaid serious involvement, guidance and selective elimination, wherever 'they' thought necessary, of the human stock, especially in our naïve and impressionable period of some two millennia ago, where they knew they could masquerade so freely as angels. It would also explain the continued presence in Earth space of a phenomena that seems so 'extra terrestrial' in nature, and the many alleged worldwide abductions which are claimed to almost always involve the removal of human genetic material.

Clearly, if an extra terrestrial presence does exist in Earth space, that had no involvement at all in the origins of humanity, there would still be abductions, and a great interest in all the many and various life forms on Earth. Also, it is obvious that 'they' would wish to probe into the genetic makeup of our body form. But if the beings, we surmise may still be observing us, are the hypothetical descendants of the creators of humanity, then the alleged removal of the genetic material in the abduction cases (if not to create an army of special hybrid beings for a specific purpose), could be assumed to be a continuing and ongoing progress check on human genetic development, perhaps looking for signs that the positive genes may be finally overcoming the negative ones so evident in our more gross and destructive behaviour pattern, and our ongoing proclivity toward destroying each other in our incessant wars and disputes all over the globe.

Clearly, the most compelling circumstantial evidence for such a seemingly preposterous, but nevertheless possible, 'alien creation' theory, is the awesome human brain, which seems such an unlikely bequest in a natural way from any apelike creatures, who have retained so little for themselves, and it openly defies the excruciatingly slow evolutionary processes, where an octopus looks pretty much the same as a fossil of its kind dated as some 125 million years old. Something, or someone, had bridged an enormous gap of evolutionary time somewhere in our past, and this 'bequest' within our sculls may well fulfil the intended objective of those that bequeathed it. The process probably began with the design of our first Moon rocket and may finish with ultimate destiny with the stars.

With all the manifestations of aerial phenomena and close encounters in the days of the biblical Patriarchs with beings just like humans, descending and coming amongst them, we may well ask that if the ancients were so privileged with so many close encounters of the third kind, why are we today not so privileged, particularly as it is evident that the phenomena has seemingly not gone away? Today, we have to make do (mostly) with encounters of just the first two kinds.

Well, the answer to that may be, that whereas the ancients had no conception of those mysterious visitors as being anything other than 'divine angels' or messengers of the Lord, such entities would now be only too aware that the masquerade is over. Today, modern cosmically aware and advanced humanity who have, as said, descended ourselves in 'pillars of fire' on our own Moon and on nearby worlds would be in a far better position than the Patriarchs to judge what they may be, and our conclusion would not be 'divine angels'. Furthermore, if these beings that were accepted by the Patriarchs as angels, were such in reality, then their powers would be awesome and they would have no need to fear any adverse reactions by humans, or feel the need to adopt a lower profile to eliminate any risk to themselves or their 'craft', brought on by panic or any 'knee jerk' reaction by humans.

In spite of our modern weaponry, any representatives of a being that could achieve that spelled out in the Genesis creation account, would wipe out any human weaponry by a similar wave of a majestic hand. Therefore, we must conclude that these entities, seemingly now keeping their distance, must have some vulnerability. If, on the other hand, they are divine representatives, some people would see a very great need for them to come amongst us again today and firmly direct human behaviour patterns. Yet they (if existing at all) remain so silent and unobtrusive that many are forced to conclude that the tantalising phenomena we do occasionally observe, are all natural occurrences that our physicists will soon explain. However, this apparent low profile is very difficult to put to a traumatised 'victim' of an alleged abduction.

If humankind are a 'creation', divine or otherwise, no one could assume 'they' would be entirely satisfied with their creation. Eventually humans will live for three, maybe four hundred years. For how long would beings with many more millions of years of evolution behind them exist? Perhaps only a few of their generations have passed by since the angels of Abraham. Could they have brought about human creation and still be overseeing the process?

CHAPTER II

'CREATOR' OR CREATOR(S)

In the first book of Moses, called Genesis it states "The Earth was without form and void and darkness was on the face of the 'deep' and that a spirit or force moved over the surface of the 'waters'.

Here we have an already formed 'deep' (or ocean) filled over a lengthy period of time due to the stated scientific or chemical processes that cause atmospheric rain to eventually fill it up. Processes that science tells us to produce H_2O on our primitive world which would also have caused the other 'waters' the Bible refers to, such as the lakes and the rivers. This suggests that far from being without form and void, the Earth was pretty much like it is today, but with a 'force' or 'spirit' moving over the waters. The scientific viewpoint that is taught to us about this force is that it was the lightning bolts and discharges into the primitive oceans that produced the amino acids, or basic building blocks of life, necessary to get the process underway.

Such experiments to prove this theory have been carried out as long ago as 60 years in a retort, simulating the assumed primitive earthly atmosphere. A few amino acids were produced and one wonders if all the correctly 'handed' and the correct number of amino acids had been produced whether spontaneous multi-cellular reproducing 'life' would have taken place causing something to finally climb out of the jar. If the scientific ability had been reached at the time of this early experiment that did enable the production of all the aforesaid prerequisites of the correct amount and appropriately 'handed' variety (there are so-called left and right handed amino acids then it is possible that a life form could have been induced. The cold scientific logic of today would tell us that the Earth, though being described as 'void' and without form that had waters (rivers and lakes) and oceanic deeps would have formed long ago and, in order to have maintained the water in liquid form would have, of necessity, sufficient atmospheric pressure and density, otherwise the waters and 'deeps' could not exist. Furthermore, gravity must also exist, in order to retain the atmospheric air molecules bounding about at a sufficiently low speed, that is, below the escape velocity of the planet so that they do not dissipate into space. Further to this, such a world would certainly not be 'without form', but would be a fully formed spherical shaped planet with oceans, rivers, lakes, air gravity and a sufficiently dense breathable atmosphere ready for beings such as ourselves, and our possible 'creators', to immediately take up residence upon.

PILLARS OF FIRE

Since the world was in the aforementioned condition we can go further and state that it must be situated in the temperate area or the habitability or ecospherial zone of a life giving star, waiting patiently for the life process to commence naturally on it, or be produced by a form of intelligence.

In the enormous 'tomorrow' of mankind, which is something in the region of four and a half billion years before our sun's behaviour patterns start to become worrisome, we ourselves will become the producers, or creators, of tomorrow, bringing the life force to the other worlds that are currently void and barren. The substance will be that which exists in our most ancient rocks, over three billion years old. Not too many tomorrows will pass by before we are actually carrying out these tasks on Venus or Mars, and the process may then have begun that we ourselves were created for in the first place.

With regard to the life forming process, we are currently, as said, rather over preoccupied with tomorrow's world and have not yet discovered how the profound process of organic multi-cellular reproductive life began, or bridged the gulf from inert inorganic matter, and with regard to human origins, the same old (but still heated) controversy reigns in places like Tennessee in the USA, between the evolutionists and the creationists over 90 years after John Scopes was almost hanged for teaching Darwinian concepts to his class, yet that event took place 50 or more years after the initial introduction of the Darwinian theory.

To return to the book of Genesis dealing with creation, Moses was clearly an educated and learned man, especially so as his upbringing was of high standing and allegedly took place in Egypt. If, as seems to be the case, his writings were influenced by events of an earlier epoch, and he, no doubt, had access to the great libraries and treasure houses of knowledge so barbarically destroyed by later conquerors, he would have been influenced by philosophical works that pondered the origins of life. This seems to have been apparent in his first book of Genesis, when he wrote "And God(s)? said 'Let the Earth bring forth grass and the herb yielding seed, and the fruit tree yielding fruit after its kind, whose seed is in itself upon the Earth'". This is a clear explanation of the genetic factor, that any seed (which obviously includes the human seed) contains the genetic blueprint and ability to produce another of its kind. Science postulates that life almost certainly did originate in water and Moses certainly agreed when he wrote "Let the waters bring forth the 'moving' creature that hath life". This was a clear distinction, with emphasis on the word 'moving' from other life forms in the waters, such as seaweed or sponges and other growths, and the mysterious transition, still not fully understood, to multi-cellular reproductive life. Therefore, Moses seems to have had access to works postulating on such processes.

PILLARS OF FIRE

In the aforementioned dualistic arguments between the theologians and the biblical concept of creation, and the more scientifically orientated evolutionary concepts, is that the dogma and viewpoint of the former condensed the event that finally produced the 'moving creature', to within a seven day period, whereas the latter takes the more logical view, backed up by (we assume) fairly accurate dating processes, that a period of billions of years was necessary to produce the 'moving creature', and that life per se (if it exists anywhere else in the cosmos) is the result of an event that took place fifteen to twenty billion years ago (some astrophysics by now speculate only 12 billion).

The colossal event of the so-called Big Bang produced the first generation stars, which had to explode in their turn in order to produce the atomic particles from which everything is made, including 'moving creatures' such as ourselves, made, as we are of 'star stuff'. Every atom in our body was once contained in a star. We may now understand the funeral expression 'dust to dust'. The dust being stardust that permeates the universe, and exists on earth that man was created from. A sizeable portion of the life of Moses was spent in the wilderness with the Hebrew peoples being led by 'angels' with their 'pillars of fire' and 'pillars of cloud, patiently lighting the way for them, which seems to be the supervision of some lengthy population distribution programme. Moses had plenty of time for reflection and study and no doubt at least one of his camels was well laden with chosen documents, brought along in exodus. Although Moses did experience doubt, dissent and uncertainty from the Hebrews during the difficult times when many wished they had stayed in Egypt, they must have listened quite a few times to the teaching and lectures of Moses, their leader, in verbal fashion before Moses wrote the Genesis account (since Moses died before they entered their 'promised land' he must have been writing it during their lengthy journeying in the wilderness). Yet there doesn't seem to be any dissent, questioning or uncertainty with regard to certain questionable writings that found their way into Genesis. This is particularly evident with regard to a certain puzzling phrase that still remains in its original form. The Hebrew people (unlike other various earthly people, such as the Babylonians, then the ancient Greeks and the Romans with numerous 'gods') worshipped one divine creator 'god' or Yahweh. Therefore, it seems strange that no questions or concern over the much quoted phrase 'Let us make men in our image', that clearly implies a group of beings or 'gods', and not a single creator, were made. But of course, the Hebrews in the desert where chastised and vilified for creating graven images and diverting from the teachings of there being only one divine God, or supreme deity, the creator of all things.

If Moses did live as long as we are taught, then he had plenty of time to rectify or explain such writings, or modify them to clear up such assumed queries. It seems that all those centuries rolled by before books on 'ancient astronauts' began appearing in the 1960s that highlighted such anomalies.

In spite of all the feastings and the offerings of sacrificial lambs and so forth in the texts and biblical writings, the creation account by Moses seems to indicate that the first men were created as vegetarians. Genesis says "God said, 'Behold, I have given you every herb bearing seed which is upon the face of the Earth, and every tree in which is the fruit of a tree yielding seed, to you it shall be for meat'. Clearly, this not only applied to mankind but to all creatures as the next paragraph goes on to say 'and to every beast of the Earth and to every fowl of the air and to everything that creepeth upon the Earth, wherein there is life I have given every green herb for meat'. The aforesaid enquiry and questioning of Moses and the teachings most certainly should have occurred as a result of the story of the first humans on the face of the Earth, that is, Adam and Eve, who the people were taught, and the Bible still teaches us today, had two sons, yet their mission was to become the progenitors of the human race. Further complications set in with the slaying of Abel by Cain. The drama involved in the creation story centres around the appearance of Adam and Eve and, although a wife appears later for Cain in the Bible prior to the onset of the greats 'begatting', no mention of her being specifically created appears.

The people of the ancient east must have been aware of the three distinct racial types making up the populations of the Earth, that is, Caucasian, Negroid and Asian, and pondered on the (still undetermined) racial origins of Adam and Eve. They must also have surely considered the origins of humanity to have been based on incestuous relationships and inbreeding, unless a regular supply of created wives to the male offspring were constantly produced, or created in 'Eden'.

We are able to determine a very rough location for the Garden of Eden, whose actual position seems to have been written about with the intention of being purposely vague. There are a few clues given to us in the writings of Genesis, especially where the River Euphrates is mentioned, but Eden is not mentioned as being in any specific location alongside or in close proximity to any city to town subsequently mentioned in the Bible. To say east or west of the Euphrates would be as vague as saying it was east or west of the Rive Nile, another very long river also flowing through a large land mass and specifically of interest when the land of Ethiopia comes into the picture, which the 'Blue Nile', does enter. Genesis states 'And a river went out of Eden to water the Garden, and from thence it was parted and became into four heads, Euphrates, Pison, Gihon and Hidekel'. Strangely, Gihon is said to encompass the whole land of Ethiopia and now we are in East Africa there are also many other rivers in that land. However, with Ethiopia coming into the picture, we have an enormous tract of land to consider; stretching from the Rivers Tigress and

Euphrates in a south westerly direction across the Arabian Desert, then ultimately, across the Red Sea into Ethiopia and our search becomes likened to that of Eldorado, Shambala, Camelot, the Ark of the Covenant or the Holy Grail. Clearly, as the biblical characters, such as Moses and Abraham (that we can identify), were Middle Eastern in origin, they are naturally going to assign the location of Eden to their own lands and, since it would (unless being a remote oasis) be near their main river sources, then we could consider, in this regard, a possible area, clearly depicted in 'The Bible Alive' (Harper Collins 1993), that shows four separate rivers in a roughly X shaped configuration, but they are only interlinking junctions of the two main rivers Tigress and Euphrates. They are shown on a map of the world of the Patriarchs in the above book and, if indicating the possible area of 'Eden, then this would place it down near the Kuwait border and dividing the countries of Iraq and Iran.

When drawing on the vast amount of data that must have existed in the filing system of Moses, with all the much older texts listing all the biblical characters, their names, their offspring and the enormous life spans they seem to have enjoyed, and whom begat whom, the germ, or idea, of a human creation zone having existed somewhere, seems apparent. It seems, on face value, to be a clever 'ploy' in mentioning the Euphrates as a clue to the whereabouts of Eden, then not only mentioning three other rivers that are unidentifiable, but throwing Ethiopia into the equation also, so that we have an area from the Mountains of Turkey to the Gulf of Iran and west to Ethiopia to consider. The first book of Genesis, with reference to Eden says "And the Lord God planted a garden eastward in Eden". So this would strengthen the assumption of it being located between the Euphrates and the Tigris. Mesopotamia encompassed all of the present day Iraq and the word is said to be of Mesopotamian origin meaning 'plain' or 'steppe land'.

However, bearing in mind the foresaid proclivity toward assigning the location of Eden to their own lands by the Patriarchs which is natural enough in the need to relate their own existence to the creation 'legend', if the fantastic proposition is possible, offered also in many other works, that the racial memory or legend of Eden is based on an extra terrestrial 'creation zone' here on Earth, then a far more desirable location, such as a large island cleared of serious predators may (for example) have been seen as a much more sensible zone than a small desert oasis. Such a location would have the obvious advantage of a sea barrier all around and the ability to prevent the created entities from wandering away until their creators were good and ready to transport them to the various locations, to "replenish the Earth", as mentioned in the Genesis creation story. The Eskimos are said to have a legend that their original ancestors were transported to the region in 'great metal birds'.

The god (or gods) of the human creation zone, seemed to be extremely adept at producing many different life forms rolling off in almost production line profusion and seemed to be masters of genetic creation. Or could we consider another interesting idea or possibility, and that is, the creator(s) may have brought with them to Earth many life forms indigenous to their own world, in the form of frozen reproductive genetic material, or may be living embryos, if they had discovered the secrets of successful freezing and thawing of living cellular tissue, and produced life forms here on Earth that could survive quite happily in an earthly environment. If they did adapt well to our earthly conditions, they may have survived and proliferated, remaining 'each until their kind', which certainly seems to be the case with our distinct lack of 'transitional' species, and particularly the strict code that confounds the evolutionary theories and prevents chaotic change or inter-breeding, that is, the chromosome count or pattern that determines each individual species controlled by the rigid pattern in their DNA molecule to produce another of their kind.

In the Genesis story of creation, God (or 'gods') "Brought each creature unto Adam to see what he would call them, and whatsoever Adam called every living creature, that was the name thereof". If the creator(s) were 'gods', and not God, then instead of telling Adam the lengthy and complicated list of possible extra terrestrial names for the creatures that were produced, 'they' may have felt that Adam would remember them all far more easily if he himself supplied their names.

After creating the first human, Adam the creator(s) appeared to carry out some form of cloning process by removing material (not necessarily a complete rib) from Adam to produce another of his kind, where only the gender is changed to provide a wife for him. It is easy to talk glibly of 'genetic reproduction', but we could be considering creatures that were thousands, or possibly millions, of years ahead of us, when people were being 'bled' by the physicians (to cure practically everything).

Today medical science is working on the shortly to be achieved possibility of cellular production of a human heart in a laboratory? What will be possible in just another century at the current pace of advancement?

Surely, it is reasonable to assume that any creative intelligent entities from a similar planetary environment as ourselves which, by sheer computation or 'weight of numbers', there must be a great multitude, would be similar in genetic makeup to ourselves? If the atoms and molecules that have come into existence, and our current list of elements from exploding stars are all finite, then creatures with a similar metabolism as ourselves arriving to 'create in their own image' is not really such a fantastic supposition particularly if such creatures had found other worlds with multi-cellular life forms on them and had a vast array of knowledge and samples of all the various genetic groups found thereon, to experiment with and blend with other similar life forms. We do this with some of our plants to produce other varieties and the same analogy could be seen in the earlier alchemist's work of experimenting with and blending various chemical elements together. Also, our earlier alloying experiments with metals to produce tougher or less brittle iron, by varying the amounts of carbon added, and so forth.

All these processes could have taken place on other worlds millions of years ago. Why do men have nipples, and why does nature sometimes 'slip back', so to speak, and produce a genuine hermaphrodite, or produce unfortunate people who have to live their lives in confusion, unless a specific sex change operation is carried out to ensure a firm position within a definite gender? The delicate balance achieved in the possible creation experiment remains, apparently, quite precarious.

In the creation story of Genesis we can clearly read an account of Adam being put under an anaesthetic before an operation. A 'deep sleep' was induced in Adam and the creator(s) took the genetic material and 'closed up' the incision.

If such a hypothetical supposition that human kind were created by extra terrestrial (planetary) beings it would be a most profound revelation, or discovery, to us at any rate, but such advanced entities may view such activity as commonplace and their reason for existence, and such activity may have been carried out by generations of their forebears and indeed, may actually be carried out by humans in some remote point in our future. Such operations would have to be ongoing for generations after the original event, by observing the outcome of their genetic 'blending' and mental activity of their 'creations'. The signs of mental and intellectual advancement and development and constant observations of the behaviour patterns would have to be carefully monitored for a long period of time and the current abductions alleged to be occurring may all be part of that ongoing plan. In short, 'they' have taken on a responsibility for human behaviour patterns.

Early on, in such a hypothetical creation programme, there would be simple tests for early mental development, such as strength of character, for example. The signs of their bequest of intellect would be searched for by the 'creators'. What can we deduce from a 'tree' of knowledge and a 'tree' of good and evil? It does seem more than a coincidence that they were seemingly purposely positioned, as the creation story tells us, in the 'middle, of the garden, rather than haphazardly around the perimeter. It would seem that they were positioned where they would be obvious.

We could use the analogy of a sign saying 'wet paint' that seems to draw people towards it, and some to actually touch it. Such a purposeful positioning of these 'trees' implies that they were meant to be approached and that it was desirable for the creations to be attracted to them for the aforesaid test procedures, and their obvious and purposeful location would act like a magnet to beings bestowed with curiosity, the motivation for learning in a creature with intelligence.

The fantastic combination of curious enquiry and superb creativity is the reason for all human advancement. When reading of these 'trees', whatever they were, one gets the distinct impression that the creator(s) would have been very disappointed if Adam and his mate Eve had not noticed, reacted to or approached these 'trees' at all and, although Adam's actions in submitting to the temptation test and removing an information sphere? Or 'apple' from the 'tree', ensured that he was dispatched perhaps more quickly than he might have otherwise been to 'subdue and replenish the Earth'. This was surely the first part of the reason for this creation of intelligent entities in the first place. We certainly couldn't envisage the creator(s) subduing the Earth and doing all that tilling of the Earth with the sweat of their brows themselves while their creations roamed leisurely about the Garden eating fruit all day.

In Genesis, the god(s) said "Behold the man is become as one of us". Another strange usage of the plural implying a 'group' of creators. The meaning of this phrase, used after Adam had succumbed to the curiosity and enquiring test could equally be interpreted as meaning "Behold the man has the intelligence and enquiry as expected as a result of our genetic material supplied to him".

Who (or what) was the 'serpent', utilised possibly by the creator(s) to motivate or prompt Adam during his assumed intelligence test? Legends of serpent beings abound throughout earthly mythology, often connected with cosmic creation myths, and are not usually referred to as evil, but as wise and all-knowing and quite often have 'cosmic connections. The serpent, or lowly snake, in Moses' version of human creation, may have been a denigration down through the period from the original creation myths Moses may have drawn heavily upon when compiling his own version of the event.

Almost every nation on Earth has its creation myths, all having one central common denominator in that men were 'made' by 'gods'. The Bible could be viewed as the creation myth of the Christians. If human kind were divinely created in the manner described in the Christian Bible, it certainly would not have been a recent or 'fresh' enough event for Moses to have such a meticulous account of it to have to write about, and he may well have selected, or picked out, the best from the many various legends, and then set down his rather precise and detailed biblical account.

Although certain circumstantial evidence can be called upon (which will be looked at later) for the possible existence of a clever and creative human race of antediluvian peoples surely none of the creation legends can go back further than a period of 50 – 100 thousand years ago, or before the appearance of Cro-Magnon men. Which may be the whole hinge pin of all the creation stories, as then Adam and Eve would have been most unattractive created entities, assuming the description in all those anthropological drawings depicting Neanderthal 'men' are accurate. If we go back much, much further to the era of the Hominids, they certainly would not be representatives that could be viewed as 'made' in the image of the creator(s).

The obvious conclusion to all this is the being who was made in the image of the creator(s) was the Cro-Magnon entity. Tall, erect intelligent and artistically creative. This being could be said to be the only true human ancestor as we have little, if anything, in common with the Neanderthal entity, or even less with the much earlier Hominids. Cro-Magnon, in spite of his 'sudden' appearance, would look pretty much the same as humans do today. Could this period 50 – 100 thousand years ago have been the time of the great creation programme?

This amazing, monumental leap forward in time that had required previously all the hundreds of millions of years from the so-called Cambrian explosion of species (likened to some primordial creation event in itself) of 600 million years ago, to produce the final entity (prior to Cro-Magnon) that is, Neanderthalensis Sapiens, only to become an entity earmarked for extinction, as it is a fact that Neanderthal later finds showed him apparently retrogressing, and he did, in fact, die out. Yet the Cro-Magnon men appear, in relation to this enormous time span, almost overnight. Cro-Magnon defied all the evolutionary perquisite of excruciatingly slow, plodding, selective processes and almost proves the case for 'creation', divine or otherwise, and if a divine God did create the Earth, some four and a half million years ago in order to agree with the scientific proclamations for the event, then he waited some 11 to 15 billion years after creating the universe (in order to fit in with another scientific assessment) before creating the Earth, together with the rest of the solar system, and another four billion years or so before creating people. None of this fits in very neatly with the concept of a divine creation event, where the story has everything being wrapped up in a week and yet it still remains in the same form in the Bible today.

However, the plain fact remains that almost eighty generations of people have accepted the story in Genesis for human creation without question since

2,000 years ago alone, and one supposes, since the Bible attributes the writing of Genesis to Moses, that almost another forty to fifty generations accepted it *before* that date. It is only the last few generations that have been subjected to scientific advancement and astrophysical data, coupled with a renewed concept of the creation event, that have been under the most pressure and regard to their beliefs in the biblical account, yet science has not provided all the answers by any means.

They cannot explain where the mass of hydrogen came from in the first place. If any *one* huge orange star can produce the theoretical 'black hole' by collapsing in on itself after a supernovae where not even light can escape, when there are countless billions of stars, how could a mass that must have contained all the material for all those stars have exploded in the first place?

We might have the answers by now if our zealousness for destroying written knowledge had been matched by a will or proclivity toward preserving it. Who *were* all those writers that produced so much data that a good *six months* of concentrated effort in burning it all didn't quite get the job done? It is said the people travelled from all corner of the known world to study in the Alexandrian library. When referring to the lack of intelligent enquiry by the Hebrews of Moses' writings, assuming he *did* preach some of it to his followers around the camp fire at sometime or during all that desert wandering, another point that would surely have raised a few eyebrows would have been the apparently enormous longevity of some of the biblical Patriarchs and characters written about by Moses in Genesis books one and two. Abraham himself, died fairly young at 175 years old, compared to some of his predecessors and successors. Adam, having lived allegedly for 900 years and Methuselah and Noah also living for centuries, should surely have prompted at least some questions or enquiry in the recipients of such stories about their predecessors, especially as they would have observed people coming to their end during the forty years in the wilderness after quite normal life spans.

The question now arises, if the amazing assumption has any truth at all, in that other world intelligence created humanity, then their long evolution and advancement necessary for them to carry out such activity, did 'they' possibly live for many hundreds of years and pass on this longevity in their bequest of their genetic material in their human creations?

In Genesis what was the 'tree' of life that the creator(s) were so worried about with regard to their created entities taking from it and becoming like them 'to live forever'? With regard to the expulsion of Adam from the Garden, in a scenario where we choose to view the Garden of Eden as a genetic creation centre, producing human beings by the actions of other world intelligence, the creations leaving the Garden would surely be the ones seen as fit and ready to

PILLARS OF FIRE

do so, and those retained would be kept for further observation and tests for developing intelligence becoming apparent. Therefore, the cherubim's with the revolving 'sword' mentioned in Genesis would possibly be to prevent entities leaving prematurely than attempting to return. Were the cherubim some kind of robotic entity? What of the flaming 'sword' turning this way and that? It sounds like a good description of a revolving laser beam.

When the first created entities left the creation centre, surely the creator(s) did not wind up the programme and just leave everything to Adam and his wife to get things going? As said, although no mention of a wife being created for Cain, the only remaining offspring of Adam and Eve (after murdering his brother) was referred to by Moses, one did appear for him that, we must assume, emanated from this same creation centre. Furthermore, the actions of Cain in murdering his own brother should surely have seen his suitability as a future 'progenitor' as questionable, and the creator(s) should have seen the need for him to have entered the Garden for some neurological 'adjustment'. Is this where the hypothetical creators made their biggest mistake? By not getting things right at the very onset of their programme, it became necessary for their assumed descendants, still observing the ongoing results of the original creation plan, to eliminate all those malfunctioning occupants of Sodom and Gomorra? And Babylon even more so in the dramatic flooding of the earth, in the days of Noah?

The same negative traits in the human neurological processes still equal and retard our more positive attributes and, although being no stronger than them, but certainly in equilibrium, hold back the advancement of humanity toward true civilisation enormously. Did the assumed other world creator(s) simply theorise that all the negative genes would be quickly consumed? What we could view as a failure or flaw in their operations would certainly be more indicative of fallible entities, rather than a divine infallible being.

The aforesaid wife for Cain appears in Genesis where Cain 'knew' his wife a (popular biblical expression for having sexual intercourse). At this point, Cain was in the Land of Nod, somewhere to the east of Eden. In Genesis Cain was marked for extinction by the creator(s) (remindful of the Auschwitz Tattooings also marking people to extermination), and he 'went out' to the Land of Nod after the slaying of his brother Abel.

Before the murdering of Abel, Cain and his brother, together with their parents, the original created entities, must all have resided in fairly close proximity to the original creation zone of Eden, and this is verified in the offerings of gifts to the creator(s) that caused all the trouble eventually for Cain (and even more so for Abel). How did they get back *into* the garden to offer such gifts? Clearly, they were living close by and would have been tilling the earth with the sweat of the brow in fairly close proximity to the Eden creation centre.

If we analyse the train of events leading up the slaying of Abel by his brother Cain, more circumstantial evidence for the original creators likelihood of being 'other world intelligence' rather than a divine creator, appears. Clearly, the creator(s) were happy enough to allow their creations and their offspring to continue in adulation and subservient worship of them, which included the offerings of gifts. However, at first glance, the creator(s) seemed to have handled the event rather unwisely that ultimately led to the slaying of Abel. Even moderately competent parents would ensure that when their offspring (or in other words, their *own* creations) offered gifts to them, that they would give out equal praise to each of them, quite regardless of the quality, price or worth of the gifts so offered, and not deride one and praise the other, and it was this kind of action on behalf of the assumed creator(s) that provoked the hostility and rage in Cain, that most certainly, though indirectly, led to the typically human reaction of jealousy and fury in Cain that caused the subsequent killing of his brother Abel.

Firstly we could take the view that an all-knowing divine creator who would have all the wisdom of the world and would not have handled it that way in coldly stating 'one gift was inadequate and one was acceptable'. *But*, emotional, sympathetic qualities in the present normal state of human mental advancement *would* cloud the issue of pure logic, even to the point of telling lies out of sympathy and regard for the feelings of the person offering the inadequate gift. Then, and to emphasise the possibility of the creator(s) being 'other world superior advanced entities', they may deal in pure logic, where a being on their own world would expect to be dealt with in pure logic, and in this situation an 'other world' Cain would simply accept the statement that his gift was inadequate and immediately go away and attempt to improve upon it, without any human reactions of anger, jealousy and rage, which could be viewed as mental immaturity in humans.

And such high advanced creators, so used to dealing with beings on their own level on their own world, may have to strain enormously to come down to the mental level of humans when dealing with them, much like our attempts to understand the emotional needs of a monkey.

In their role as progenitors of the human race, Adam and Eve had yet another son they called Seth, making it more difficult for them to create a favourable situation for the onset of all the begetting that is so meticulously listed in the Old Testament. Of course, this presumed the view that a system of in-breeding and incestuous copulation and production of offspring was intended of the original creations for the process of multiplying, but this may not have been the case and a production line of female entities may have been underway by the creators (though not mentioned in the Bible) to, as said previously, industriously provide all the wives for Cain and then Seth, and anyone else that needed one. After Cain 'knew' his wife and she gave birth to Enoch, as soon as he was old enough to be able to appreciate it, his father Cain soon got busy building him a city, at this point of human procreation, this city would have been more akin to a ghost town, so few entities were around to occupy it. Furthermore, this implies the necessity of knowledge of working in stone and woodwork, and of town planning and administration, and skills of many others that would have to be normally involved in such a project. Where did Cain acquire all this knowledge when, only going back to his own parents, the only things they were good at was tilling the Earth with the sweat of their brow and the possible manufacture of crude dwellings, and regarding this city only six entities, Adam, Eve, Cain, Seth, Enoch and Cain's wife existed. However, this is the time in the Bible of the onset of the 'begattings' and how Moses could be so detailed in all the names and characters, where they died and at what age, is quite amazing. The great begattings go on and up to the time of Noah and his offspring.

As formerly stated, other earlier accounts of a similar character to Noah exist, obviously with a different name, but having the same central theme of being chosen, together with their families, to be saved from the wrath of the creator(s), who now began seemingly, to regret ever having started the human procreation programme, and decided to wipe it all out, save for a few entities who appear to be functioning within the accepted parameters that were originally intended.

And so the great culling programme, or separation of the malfunctioning human creations, begins which certainly would not be the last of such activity where the creator(s) decide, coolly and calmly to wipe out, or terminate humanity, 'en masse'.

Clearly, the hope of the 'terminators' was to allow those specially selected entities (who were allowed to live on) to begat suitable and like-minded offspring – shades of the 'master race' syndrome. Were the Nazi medical experiments, or the more recent 'ethnic cleansing' that occurred in the Bosnian War definitely inherited racial memories of these far off events manifesting their symptoms of striving to produce racial superiority in the human stock?

How can we accept a divine creator who had his own son later on in the biblical writings, uttering such statements as 'love thy neighbour', 'turn the other cheek', 'forgive them, they know not what they do', 'love thine enemies', and so forth, being seen as a cold blooded mass murdered? 'the possibility' is promoted by just such actions as these, that the perpetrators may well have been super-advanced, cold, calculating 'other world' creators, who *did* view humanity as 'property' and felt quite at liberty to eliminate, or save, anyone they felt required such treatment. In any case, they probably would take this somewhat easier path of mass termination rather than adopting the tiresome process of bringing such an obviously large number of malfunctioning human creations back through the system, a bit like a motor company recalling *all* their models for fault diagnosis and subsequent rectification. If the hypothetical creators left Earth 'between missions', as it were, particularly at enormous velocities, exceeding light speed, a very long time could pass by *on Earth* but not for them, and the population on Earth *would* be greatly increased when they returned.

Certain writers have postulated on the afore-mentioned antediluvian races, or people existing before the flood, processing great knowledge and advancements, who were possibly genetically quite different from present humanity, but all their advancements and achievements were swept away and now lay buried under layers of silt, and people living for centuries now no longer exist. Some writers have gone so far as to say that they may even have achieved the art of flying, and even nuclear weapons and their delivery. There are earthly legends that speak of flying craft; even how to construct them. Writings once viewed as fables, scrutinised by a modern eye, now sound like the delivery of atomic missiles upon the unfortunate heads of the enemy. Gold models from ancient time periods, looking and performing in wind tunnel test just like aircraft, are subjected to the 'can't be, so they aren't' diagnosis. The afore-mentioned vitrified green glass substance so familiar in nuclear test areas, have been found all over the globe.

Artefacts, clearly manufactured and produced, have been found in coal seams and blasted out with quarry stone from time periods long into the past. Ribbed boot prints, clearly showing a manufactured sole have been found in ancient rock. Dr. Clifford L. Burdick, an Arizona geologist, is shown adjacent to page 112 in 'Secrets of the Lost Races' (Nel) by Rene Noorbergen, showing plaster casts of a dinosaur, and human 15" footprints found together in a paluxy river bed in Texas, totally decimating evolutionary timescales and assumptions.

The most profound reason suggested for massive wipe-out and flooding holocausts, apart from purposeful actions by off-Earth intelligence, is a very traumatic event having possibly occurred, and that is the possible tilting of the Earth's axis to its present position of 23° and written legends exist of the Sun spinning around and the sky 'falling into the sea', which would appear to be happening to someone who was observing the event, but they have had to have done their observing from a high point to have lived to record it and avoid the subsequent flooding.

Did this possible difference in the makeup or metabolism of the ancients allow them to live for a huge time span, compared to modern humanity? Is this why the Hebrews failed to question the immense ages of the Patriarchs as related in such a matter of fact way by Moses in Genesis? Were they quite familiar with stories of the 'antediluvian' peoples?

Nobody seems capable of explaining the utter mysteries of the past and it is easier to ignore them. When we speak of items lying unclassified in duty museum basements, that is exactly what happened in the case of a model plane, classified as a bird, that was found when Dr. Kahil Messiah, an Egyptologist, was cleaning out a museum basement of old artefacts. It was an item discovered in a tomb near Saqqara in Egypt in 1898. The doctor had been a model plane enthusiast and recognised its aerodynamic 'aircraft like' features of wings, tail plane stabiliser and fin with a pronounced 'anhedral', an aircraft designer's option for enhanced lift. A committee was formed of specialists who immediately recognised the many features of it used in aircraft design and the 'bird' is thought to be over 2,000 years old and it 'flies' perfectly when hand launched. This artefact was lucky enough to have been subjected to the treatment al the 'ooparts' or out of place artefacts should be subjected to, until an acceptable classification of their real identity is forthcoming.

We cannot do this, unfortunately, with the high quality steel cube with the convex ends and machined groove in it, found in a coal seam in Austria, as only a wooden replica of it now exists, the original having gone missing. But records of its original find are well documented in the Austrian museum.

Could we then conjecture, that the antediluvian races manifested a much higher standard of their possible 'bequest' of intellect by the creator(s) than we give them credit for? Evidence seems to continually appear that confounds the original perception we held of the ancients as grunting cave dwellers, even of the Stone Age. Many cave bottoms have been evaluated and examined without a trace of evidence indicating any human occupation, but finely built stone dwellings of the period have been found, even having signs of 'aspect' or planning that is, facing a river or toward the Sun, even evidence of the Stone Age peoples having knowledge and awareness of cement and mortar and utilising it in their constructions.

Metal implements would be difficult to find from such an ancient period for obvious reasons of oxidisation and dissolving back to what they were in the first place. However, ancient copper mines have been found all over the world, where even the indigenous natives of the area have nothing to say about them in their legends. One example of such a find is in Northern USA, in the Lake Superior area, a known copper rich zone. It would appear that even the indigenous native American Indians have no knowledge of their origins and their legends tend to go far back into the past.

Some of these mines of unknown origin appear to have had good organisation and transportation methods, as no evidence of their products is found in any region out to a thousand miles away from the source, and no indications of the workers having lived or settled in the surrounding area, with no bones or skeletons indicating burials, yet thousands of tons of ore had apparently been dug out from the sites by an obviously sizeable workforce – surely a strange thing?

With regard to the various legends of global flooding, the fossil record speaks out plainly that massive flooding affected at least parts of the globe. Fish fossils, for example, that had no time to decompose or disperse after death before being entombed and sealed in forever in hardened material that was once mud. That the flood was worldwide seems to be universally rejected. That there was a flood (or floods) is universally accepted and the afore-mentioned fossil evidence seems to bear this out. As for the biblical account, it is suggested that Moses simply copied the earlier Babylonian version, but changed certain factors, such as the name of the main character to Noah from the Chaldean, 'Xisuthros', and the description and dimensions of the survival vessel, or 'ark'. The geological record also clearly indicates widespread flood occurrences, as a matter of fact, 75% of the Earth's land surface has sedimentary layers. Rene Noorbergen in 'Secrets of the Lost Races' (Nel 1980) states 2448 BC as the traditional biblical chronological date for the flood event.

Although evidence of local flooding exists in the Mesopotamian areas of the Tigris and Euphrates, the biblical date for the estimated time of the flood causing the waters to be swirling up around the peaks of the Turkish mountains, is almost certainly wrong. Why? Because (for one example) the older pyramids of Egypt would have been *already standing for at least 150 years,* along with the rest of the fantastic Egyptian culture and meticulous recording process and evidence of inundation would surely be evident in the sides of the pyramidal structures and effigy such as the Sphinx and, in an area such as the Nile occupies, they would have been among the first affected.

The original flood that instilled itself into legends, must have occurred *much* earlier than any biblical estimates, certainly well prior to the first Egyptian dynasty, a date on which the 'experts' cannot even agree, and ranges up to 3,000 BC. However, the basic ingredients of some kind of purposeful mass annihilation of large numbers of the human race is retained in such documents as the Bible, that many accept word for word. With regard to Sodom and Gomorra, for example, the occupants are wiped off the face of the Earth literally, it seems, 'in a flash'. There is no mention of the aftermath, of relatives weeping and wailing and gnashing of teeth, of mass burials and funerals, or of disease or decay, with vultures and buzzards descending on the town. The occupants were simply obliterated with no further mention of them occurring.

As said, with regard to all the flood legends, history can produce more than one Noah. However, the curious thing is that the writings of Moses are so explicit his 'sons and heirs', and lists meticulously the descendants and how long they lived, and so forth, and one is compelled to assume that Moses was writing about a real person, and this is reinforced by giving him more human qualities, such as getting drunk in his vineyard, and so forth.

If the extreme longevity and apparent technological level that caused all the head scratching with those 'ooparts' out of place artifacts and geological discoveries further enlightening us with regard to the ancients, we could assume that any special genetic qualities they may have inherited from the creators may have been destroyed along with them when the creator(s) decided to 'start again', so to speak. However, we still have problems, because Noah himself, who obviously, in accordance with the biblical story, had the ability to build a ship the size of an ocean-going liner single handed, and was begatting children at 500 years old, then going on to live to be 950 years old he had to be possessed or unique qualities. Clearly then, as Noah is said to have survived to start the human race all over again, any special genetic qualities he would have had would continue to manifest themselves in the 'new breed', that is, his many descendants.

Lamech, Noah's father, lived himself for 777 years and the Genesis account of Noah and his line of descendants, certainly seems to be saying that Noah begat his offspring Shem, Ham and Japheth when he was in his fifth century of existence. Clearly, if these beings did ever exist, they were very special people indeed. If their creations had such special qualities with all that longevity, how long did the creator(s) live?

With all the centuries of human procreation and multiplication on Earth, both succeeding and ante-dating the termination programmes or flood epics, the creator(s) still remained on Earth, or at least successive generations of them, and if they had enormous life spans, hundreds of years could be spent in Earth space by the same entities. During the Roman Empire soldiers could spend a large part of their lives campaigning and adventuring in foreign fields, and in their day, if one lived to fifty years of age it was considered old.

Did this long campaign by the alleged creator(s) far away from 'planet heaven', or their source or origin, finally allow their standards to slip a little? If we are created in their image, then human females would not surely have appeared too unattractive to them. Another much quoted line from Genesis that

PILLARS OF FIRE

Moses was responsible for stating, "The sons of God (or the creator(s) saw that the daughters of men were fair, and they took them wives of all that they chose", and the apparent result of the creator(s) 'knowing' these daughters produced strange, uncontrolled genetic offspring, certainly with regard to their growth and stature hormones, as it goes on to say "and there were giants in the Earth in those days, …. And also after that, when the sons of (the creator(s)) came in unto the daughters of men and they bear children to them, and the same became 'mighty men', which were, of old men of renown". The biblical characters such as Moses, would have interpreted this as simply unbridled lust on behalf of the creators. Any king or important personage could take any female he chose and the relatives considered it normal, perhaps even an honour. Abraham's wife Sarah was selected out herself in this manner and Abraham passed her off as his sister a couple of times, perhaps for his own safety, which will be related in that chapter. With regard to the afore-mentioned 'giants', seemingly a freak genetic offspring, perhaps another interpretation could be put on the event.

Were they simply, early recorded female abductions, perhaps for the removal of their eggs, for a further life form experimental programme? This seems more likely than the hypothesis of such advanced entities letting their rigid standards slip like shipwrecked sailors chasing native women. Far into the future, human beings may regard sexual intercourse as an occurrence during the savage part of their history and may wonder how their ancestors could have copulated like the animals do. They may now view it as a primitive distasteful process. They may simply select the number of, the height, the gender, physical prowess and IQ from something like a modern day car brochure, and their science does the rest.

Could we conjecture that these, possibly specially bred entities, were created for a specific purpose or special projects? Although the Hebrews in their desert wanderings did, according to Moses' accounts of the events, do many battles with them, or with the giants as the 'leader' of the enemy force, they do occasionally pop up in later generations of the Hebrews, such as in the time of David and Goliath.

However, accounts and legends of giants do not only occur in the Mesopotamian, or biblical lands of the Earth, they appear in many earthly legends. Massive stone structures, for which the purpose of their construction remains a mystery, are present in different earthly locations, such as Tiahuanaco, for example, with no explanation of who constructed them except, perhaps, for vague reference to 'sky people' or 'gods', and many ancient Irish legends refer often to 'giants', and they also found their way into children's old fairy tales, such as 'Jack the Giant Killer', and so forth.

And so, instead of these 'giants' being the result of uncontrolled genetic mutations, they may have been part of a specific plan. They also appear to have been perhaps having fulfilled their purpose, completely obliterated, as no extraordinarily large skeletons have ever been found, except perhaps for the occasional tall, but not robust, occurrences due to possible hormonal disorders that appear from time to time. Are such occurrences in humanity, that appear now and then, occasional appearances in the dispersed gene pool evidence of this alleged ancient experimenting as part of the wider creation plan? We don't seem to witness huge, or exceptionally large, examples appearing in the other species of Earth, and humans sometimes produce the odd wonder child and other great intellects, and people (usually in the colder zones where healthier conditions exist) that live to extreme old age. When we postulate, have the 'aliens' of Abraham gone away? Why don't they move among us now? Well, for all we know, perhaps they do. The 'aliens of Abraham and Lot clearly caused little or no alarm when moving among the people of Earth of the period, and therefore, if they were adopting a pretty good disguise in the era of the Patriarchs, how clever would their abilities *now* have become in order to move amongst us totally unnoticed? Perhaps, unbeknown to us, our every discovery or technological progression is being telepathically encouraged to hasten our progress along the road to be becoming creators ourselves. They may be looking forward to 'retirement' and wish to conclude their universal duty of promoting intelligent creation in their chosen subjects, and long for us to take over, and when we do 'grow' that human heart and actually set about terra forming Mars, they may prepare themselves for the new breed to 'bear the burden of creation', which Sumerian legend states, *was* the reason for the creation of humanity in the first place.

Whichever way we choose to interpret our possible creator(s), there are two clear conclusions to it all. In the case of a divine creator, it would be confrontation, and perhaps some kind of repeat of a 'challenge by Satan', to the original creator and his power *caused* by the creators' *own* actions in giving us all the intellect in the first place. Or, in the case of other worldly intelligence producing the human kind, the aforesaid successful conclusion to the intended plan. Whoever the creator(s) were they must have a higher authority, or controlling body, such as a divine 'god the father' in a remote, mysterious 'heaven', or a large complex on some far off world controlling, or directing, their cosmic voyagers, or creators of intelligence, operating on faraway worlds. Something akin to, perhaps the NASA complex, with great memory banks detailing their cosmic voyagers' discoveries and actions in other zones of the galaxy. Could it be that the floods and catastrophes, according to the various written legends, were all purposely brought about by an intelligence greater than ours, that a significant decision was made by such a ruler, or ruling body, on a world I will call "Planet Heaven"? This seems a suitable phrase when considering the many references to such a place in connection with the strange activity that appears to have been going on in biblical times.

Put the case, that the rulers of 'Planet Heaven', when receiving all those reports for the great memory banks, began to notice that the procreation programme was going wrong – they were receiving too many reports of the 'creations' exhibiting negative, destructive, evil and warlike tendencies – then just as is recorded in Genesis the master computer that rules their decisions, states 'terminate'. After some discussion between the creator(s) with their chosen (possibly hybrid) entity we call a Patriarch, that is Noah, explicit dialogue ensues to the effect that they (the creator(s)) wish for Noah to select, together with his immediate family, a large cross-section of earthly life forms, in order to commence a repopulation of the Earth later on. We have seen that Noah was obviously a very special entity and was clearly capable of taking charge of the construction plan clearly imparted to him, to build the vessel to house all the selected forms.

Genesis confirms this special status of Noah as he was high enough to 'walk' with the creator(s). Finally (Genesis), Noah receives his explicit instructions to build the survival vessel.

Tantalising aerial photographs of a boat-like shape *have* appeared, showing a formation that may be a natural feature, but seems to have the correct dimensions that were spelled out to Noah in the Bible, based on the biblical 'cubit'. It lies high up in the Turkish mountains and serious expeditions have sallied forth to investigate it, but have been plagued with political and military obstacles. Furthermore, people *can* be found in the region that swear they were taken up the mountain in their youth and were not only shown the Ark, but climbed on to it.

And so, there is some evidence to support the notion that some remnant of a petrified hulk is still up there. Ancient wood pieces have been found that have been suggested as possible fragments from the Ark *but* as wood does not exist in such high hostile regions, it is said that these ancient timbers are from dwellings, grottos and manmade articles, such as altars, and so forth, constructed by monks on past expeditions up there. However, a will to believe in the Ark is also an acceptance of the purposeful mass termination of malfunctioning human creations, whether by aliens *or* divine angels, and to be sure, the same Mesopotamian areas *still* see oppression by military dictators, wars due to ancient hatreds and religious persuasions, *all* going entirely unpunished today. We only have to switch on our television sets to see some evidence of worldwide human failing, and man's inhumanity to man, with pathetic refugees fleeing from areas where the ability to govern wisely seems non-existent and the country's resources are squandered on weapons and wasteful conflict rather than feeding and housing the people. If we consider the descendants of the hypothetical alien creators *are* still in earth space, it is possible that their current far off 'controllers' are considering another 'termination' plan, as clearly all the other ones failed? It is entirely possible, of course, that earthly natural catastrophes have been simply blamed on the 'wrath of God' by the ancients. *Then*, the imaginative stories that found their way into the Bible would all be mere fiction, from the imagination of gifted writers, such as Moses. It has been postulated that rapid polar ice melting, even shifting of the Earth's axis, *has* occurred in the past, which *could* be attributed to the actions of 'the lord' or even of extra terrestrial 'creators', but the survivors, whose traumatic experience and accounts of the sun or the sky 'slipping into the sea', *did* survive also in legends, would, no doubt, assign the event to the 'wrath of the gods'. Certainly, the shifting of the Earth's axis, in a violent and catastrophic manner, would produce massive tidal waves and flooding but would be unlikely to wipe out *all* human habitats. Some would, therefore, survive to 'tell the tale', so to speak. An out-of-balance Earth with a mass of ice on one pole with little evident on the other could possibly cause a shift in the 'angle of tilt' of the Earth. Ancient maps, such as that of the Turkish admiral Pirie Ries much written about in the recent past, shows every cove and inlet proved to be correct by modern geophysical surveys, *now* buried under a mile of ice. If it *continues* to build up and volcanic activity, coupled with global warming, melt the northern pole, this may cause the Earth to tilt to the perpendicular, producing an Earth with no seasons. If such a thing happened it is doubtful that any earthly beings would have time to build, or receive any instructions, to build an ark the size of an ocean liner and fill it with earthly creatures. Nevertheless, and advanced alien intelligence diligently observing and studying Earth, may well be aware that such a thing could happen and may be near to the point of occurring.... Who would they pick out as the modern day Noah?... The Pope perhaps... The Archbishop of Canterbury? To warn them in advance to select out of the best to survive? There are people, of course, engaged in various scientific pursuits, such as oceanographers, geophysicists, climatologists and those qualified to compile agenda and literature for geophysical conferences and reports, that could be well aware of such a possible catastrophic scenario and, because of this, take certain precautions to save *themselves* and their families, either by taking up residence in the mountains or constructing their own survival sphere, or 'Ark', packed with survival rations and housed in a sort of makeshift garage with a quick release roof. Although television programmes, conscious about their ratings, seem to over-dramatise catastrophe scenarios, it would be unlikely that information *would* be released to the masses if any government scientific advisors stated that it was likely to happen quite soon, but those who had prepared for it *themselves* could enter their watertight vessels, after having released the garage roof catches, then wait for the waters to rise to do the rest. However, there would be survivors that would live to tell the tale as in the afore-mentioned eastern legends of the Sun 'spinning around the heavens' and the sky 'falling into the sea', and the ancient Egyptian priests relating stories of the cataclysms occurring in Earth's past to visiting Greek travellers and speaking of the Sun 'not always rising in the position it does today', and so forth.

Apart from these hypothetical survival preparations by a possible handful of people, many people existing in high mountainous areas would probably survive, but there would be no more food supplies forthcoming from below and, until the waters subsided, no more going down for the winter to lower levels with their flocks after the cool of the mountains and in this case they may also expire with little crops or the conditions to sustain them at low level, and so eventually, the only surviving Noah's would be the submarine captains at sea together with their crew, and the birds.

Has naval policy changed to allow women on submarines yet? It would not be much use with a boatful of men when trying to repopulate the Earth. What tragic irony if one came aground on the peaks of Ararat and the waters began lapping around the shores of Lake Titicaca in the Andes, an area suggested by geological evidence to have once been beach sand, and the area in question was pushed up some 12,000 feet or by an equally fantastic event a long time ago.

If such an advanced antediluvian race did become annihilated in some alleged worldwide flood (or even a Mesopotamian one), what would a serious and prolonged excavation in all those layers of silt reveal?

In Genesis Noah was sealed into the Ark by the creator(s) who, it would seem, did not wish to entrust this vital operation to Noah.... "And the Lord shut him in".... After some 150 days of water that prevailed upon the earth (presumably seawater) mentioned in Genesis it was small wonder that the creator(s) lifted the vegetarian clause in the creation doctrines written by Moses. If the flesh of animals had not been eaten they would have all starved, in which case there would have been little point in saving them. The first crops would certainly have been difficult to grow and the process would have taken quite some time to generate itself after the initial land fall.

One can recall the difficult task in trying to get even grass, the easiest of things to grow, on the land of the Towyn area of North Wales after the sea swept in to give only a relatively minor and quickly receding dashing of seawater on the land, where wind, and probably a Spring tide, arrived together to form a deadly combination. Apart from high winds blowing over some caravans, the seawater flooded relatively few houses but a lot of caravans, as in that particular part of the North Wales coast, caravans are of great multitude.

Nevertheless, heavy doses of Gypsum and careful cultivation were required to get the area looking green again.

And so, after the landing on the mountains of Ararat (not necessarily Mount Ararat) Noah and his family and the animals too, no doubt, all emerge from the Ark, but herb eaters and vegetarians they could no longer be. One supposes the animals were fed from the supplies remaining on the Ark, on which there would have had to be an enormous amount of space to store all the animal foodstuffs and of course, their own supplies. However, in Genesis it came to pass that the meat eating dispensation was granted… "That every moving thing that liveth shall be meat for you". One supposes that Noah and his group would not be too keen on eating every living thing, and those that did 'liveth', one assumes, were only those that came from the Ark.

One subject that seems to be conspicuous by its absence in Genesis is any mention of the horrors that would have been apparent to Noah and the other survivors of all the numerous and bloated human and animal corpses, many thousands of which must have been lying about on the Earth. The birds, who would be the only Earth creatures to survive if the flood has been worldwide, would not have had sufficient time to devour them all before the risk of disease became a real problem. Another consideration would be what of the creators themselves? If they had brought about this cataclysm by their own actions, they would obviously have taken measures for their own survival and would have had to evacuate their 'Eden creation centre'. Where did they go? They must have relocated somewhere. What about the moon? Certainly a good observation platform to keep an eye on what was going on with regard to their creations and their activities. It would appear that what seem to be ancient 'construction sites' have been picked out on high quality Moon photographs taken from orbit and that astronauts have used a kind of code in their two way dialogue with ground control when referring to them.

If the flood was worldwide then the only possible earthly locations would be at the Poles, not so much with regard to their observational potential, but certainly a lot nearer than the Moon.

Clearly then, the creator(s), as well as having the enormously advanced genetic scientific abilities to create humanity and other life forms to order, such as the giants, they also had supreme control over weather systems and highly advanced meteorological knowledge, which so far is a young science and not too well understood as far as earthlings are concerned. Having instigated the flooding, by means we can hardly even guess at, they must have had the ability to control, or call a halt to, the conditions causing the flood and Genesis bears this out with "A wind was *made* to pass over the Earth and the waters assuaged, the fountains of the deep and the windows of heaven were *stopped* and the rain from heaven was *restrained*. Here is the Bible telling us that beings 'not of this Earth' had not only *caused* the flood but were now taking positive actions to *restrain* it.

As said early in the work, the reference to heaven, as far as the ancients were concerned, was anywhere in an upward direction past the area of the birds and the fleecy clouds, the area we would call space or 'earth space', but the entities that moved among the biblical Patriarchs spent a lot of time 'ascending' and 'descending' from *something* in the sky which could only be some form of structured assembly or craft. Perhaps the creator(s), after their initial arrival in earth space, felt a desert area too remote for their directive actions regarding their creations, so may be a suitable island location would have been considered. However, if the original Eden *was* on the mythical island of Atlantis, they would have had quite enough of islands. On this point, if Atlantis did exist and created entities were transported out in the 'great metal birds' that the Eskimo peoples refer to in the legends of *their* ancestors' arrival, the nearby coasts of Africa and the Americas would see their share of creations arriving to start all that tilling of the Earth with the sweat of their brow. Moreover, it is said that the so called 'cave man' civilisation first appeared along the western coasts of France and Spain. Furthermore, Obsidian tools, matching those of Europe, have been found in South America, together with other similar matching constructions, which would suggest either established oceanic sea trade in the Stone Age, which seems most unlikely, or a large island influencing nearby coastal areas in activities, artefacts and the spreading of similar cultural behaviour to both sides of it.

When considering again, the possible relocation of the creator(s) operational zone, it would appear that the only other consideration would be the mountain tops. To be sure, such areas were always considered to be the 'home of the gods' by many earthly peoples, and is well established in their legends and writings, and the Bible is no exception. Moses visited Mount Sinai for his encounters with the creator(s) and certainly had his share of booming voices, flashes of light and made frequent visits up into 'their' abode where he finally returned with the directives written in stone for the future behaviour patterns of the created human entities.

To return to the aftermath of the flood. When Noah and his family, and eventually all the animals, finally left the Ark, Noah certainly had plenty of life left in him to supervise the repopulation of the Earth, living as he is said to have done for a total of nine hundred and fifty years, but of course, Noah was already 600 years old when he left the Ark. The building of the Ark itself should have taken up a large part of Genesis rather than the simple dimensions based on the cubit and telling Noah to 'pitch it within and without'. Such an undertaking should have required teams of people all working together to build such a vessel. Did Noah have his own private shipyard, something akin to Camel Lairds? The vessel was 300 cubits long. Since the biblical cubit was something like a half meter, the ship turns out to be 450 feet long, seventy five feet wide and had three separate decks, or storeys. Such a huge vessel coming aground and remaining in a high area of rarefied air means that some remnant of it should be up there somewhere, and as previously said, more than one expedition has been made to the heights of Ararat, due to the tantalising evidence said to exist indicating its presence up there somewhere.

The flood accounts from various sources may be based on a single traumatic event for the entire Earth that would most certainly affect all lands and their subsequent legends of a traumatic event that occurs at a certain time in their past where the actual cause may not be realised, with the main ingredients of the legends all concentrating on how the alleged 'chosen ones' went about the business of their survival. It is a startling consideration, and at first, before looking at the compelling circumstantial evidence, seems quite preposterous, and that is, *the arrival of our Moon.*

Analysis of the lunar material brought back by the Apollo astronauts seem to confirm that theory to the astrophysicists that the Moon was never part of the Earth, and science is warming to the possibility of the Moon being a captured body, yet cannot work out the strange celestial mechanics that would bring such a mass into a neat circular orbit rather than an elliptical one which would seem more likely. Roman historians speak of pre 'selenes', or people existing before the moon arrived in earth space in between eleven and a half and thirteen thousand years ago, and geologists will confirm some very traumatic events occurred at that time, possibly even the afore-mentioned tilting of the Earth's axial position.

Certain Greek writers have said the pre-Lunar race were 'Pelasgians', people that reside in the lands before the ancient Greeks. As said, the tricky part is to work out the delicate celestial mechanics necessary to 'capture' the Moon and bring it in to a neat circular orbit with such inertial mass and lack of any retarding methods, such as, for example, the 'burn' our returning Moon explorers utilised in order to put the command module into circular orbit. A body with the mass of the approaching Moon should have swung into an elliptical orbit. However, it arrived, severe stresses, flooding, even the aforesaid change of the axial tilt of the Earth, may have occurred. Whether our hypothetical creators utilised the event for their 'termination' programme or actually caused the event, is open to conjecture.

After the flood in Genesis, comes an enormous repeat of 'begatting', once more highlighting the vast amount of data and knowledge Moses must have had access to in order to write it all down. How did this data survive when the flood must have wiped anything and everything off the face of the Earth? There is no mention of such data being installed into the Ark, only people and animals. Whereas many ancient traditions and legends were passed down by word of mouth in olden times, surely it would have been impossible for Moses to have remembered such a huge number of people, their names, their offspring and how long they all lived, but perhaps we do underestimate the ability of the ancients. A modern nineteen year old checkout person sitting at the till, views someone of say, sixty years old, as a modern day 'ancient', but that 'ancient' can work out the items in their basket in their head if there were just a few items, whereas most young people (through no fault of their own), would rely, if not completely, on a calculator. Clearly, the reason for this is the 'old fashioned' teaching methods, removed so quickly by trendy idealists, caused the brains of future children to be denied the stimulus of mental arithmetic and the 'old fashioned' times tables, as they were called, were done away with. Whereas the afore-mentioned checkout person (also through no fault of their own) had also to rely heavily and totally on computing devices, they are surely let down if and when they fail. Furthermore, if the 'ancient' offers, say 22p with a ten pound note for items coming to six pounds 22p, the questioning glance by the checkout person shows that briefly, the significance of the 22p being offered is momentarily misunderstood, as having glanced at the ten pound note the button has already been pressed and the computer shows what change should be given.

That we are becoming a nation of button pressers is an unavoidable fact of the times, and a future heavy reliance on electronics, but to remove the stimulus of mental calculations as a very useful fallback when the buttons fail by allowing students of tender age to use calculators is beyond the wit of ordinary men.

There is evidence to suggest that initially even writing was looked upon in a derisory and suspicious way, as some people did with the initial calculator in the early days of its appearance. Seemingly, it was looked upon as a process that would undermine the mental abilities of the people who had done well without it. People who had exercised their minds by committing so much to memory, particularly with regard to their various crafts, and stored all the information in their brain cells and subsequently, without any need of writing, were able to successfully pass on their various crafts to their apprentices or successors. It would seem that certain comments were made that seemed to indicate the view that the ancients regarded writing as a step backwards rather than an advancement or advantage.

The Secrets of the Lost Races mention a work by Plato, called 'Phaedrus', where he wrote about the legend of Toth, the Egyptian god who is alleged to have discovered the use of letters and demonstrated them to King Thamus as an aid to wisdom, but the wise king judged that they would be an aid to forgetfulness and any that took it up would not be cultivating their memory, and it seems to have happened as the king prophesied as the Egyptian priests found when copying the ancient funeral texts much later without understanding their meaning and not having had the benefit of 'word of mouth', passed down explanations. To a certain extent this situation still prevails today and text books on any craft are never exhaustive, and questions still have to be asked in order to elicit the correct interpretation from the master craftsman and his ability to be able to do this is called 'experience'.

To return to Genesis, Moses as said previously, made his characters believable (whether they actually existed or not) by assigning more human qualities to them. For example, after leaving the Ark and commencing the enormous task of planting and re-foliating the Earth, Noah had created a vineyard and was found drunk there by his sons, who quite probably did not begrudge this occasional indulgence in view of all he had achieved to which they surely owed their lives. Most certainly, in the aftermath of the flood, the predatory birds would have gorged themselves abundantly on all the carrion and various corpses lying about of which there would have been a great multitude, and as there is no mention of Noah taking on the task of burying them all, the silted areas alleged to be connected with the flood saga should, in theory, contain a huge mixture of bones and skeletons in complete form of all the humans and animals that perished, together with snapped off tree branches and stones, all mixed up together. Such a situation does exist in the far north where huge mounds of mammoth bones have been found mixed up with the aforesaid material, but this may have been due to the earlier cataclysmic event, previously mentioned, of some 12,000 years ago, when herds of mammoth were swept along to their deaths in a massive flooding event that could have been relative to the aforesaid shifting of the Polar axis, the coming of the Moon, or perhaps both. Such huge animals would have required a massive forceful torrent to shift them along, so why where no human corpses evident? Humans did hunt them for food and use their tusks to fashion into weapons, surely a strange thing.

Although there is a distinct absence of human bones among the mammoth remains, the mammoths certainly seemed to meet their demise in a horrifying manner and humans must have been involved or at least witnessed, such a catastrophe. These northern areas are termed the 'Ivory Islands' and are situated north of Siberia. It has been well documented that some of the mammoths have been found with their last meal of still undigested foodstuff containing buttercups, and this seems a clear indication that before being deeply enough frozen to prevent cellular breakdown of their flesh (the reason food has a fridge life unless 'flash frozen'), they stood grazing in a temperate zone. This is quite profound as it seems to indicate an immediate transportation to a frozen northern zone, and what else could do this (and keep them frozen) but an immediate tilt of the Earth carrying them abruptly to a northern area?

After the saga of the flood, as related by Moses and the aforesaid rather large list of the descendants of Noah, Genesis (still with the first book) stated 'That the Earth had one common language'. When Moses referred to the 'Earth' are we to assume he meant the Earth of only the ancients spreading out from Mesopotamia, where after most if not all of the writings in the Old Testament refer to? Moses would have been well preoccupied in the leading of the Hebrews through the wilderness and did, in fact, die before the Hebrews were settled, so clearly he had not time to go off round the world to see what language all the countries were using.

Theoretically, of course, if humanity did spread out around the world from the area of the Turkish mountains or Ararat, there was a huge continent all around and one common language would spread far and wide, but certainly not around the entire world. Obviously the Oriental races of China, Japan and the Polynesian races do not come into the picture, having their own roots legends, writing (which is so distinctive) and their own history. The same also applied to the Negroid peoples. However, the point in making this statement about the common language allows us neatly to lead into the story of the tower of Babel. It is at this point where the Bible starts getting interesting with regard to the onset of direct action, appearance and close encounters by the creator(s) or 'angels'.

There are such a numerous amount of references throughout the Bible of 'angels', above or 'angels' coming down on pillars of cloud, as to make it fairly obvious that the creator(s) did require and utilise some form of transport to allow them to either rise up, come down or otherwise appear to the Patriarchs and others in all those 'close encounters of the third kind'.

And so, the creator(s) now begin to take on a more obvious profile and, seemingly, become more concerned and involved in the activities of humanity. With regard to the tower of Babel, clearly they were quite upset when they heard (how did they 'hear' of it?) of their creations building this tower to impertinently invade their abode. One can easily form an impression of the creator(s) rising up from their safe mountainous havens on planetary observation missions, and watching the antics of their creations. The tower of Babel account in Genesis does make it quite clear in "The Lord came down to see the city and the tower". Would a divine Lord need to 'come down' to see what was occurring? We are taught that the Lord sees and knows everything, even our most secret thoughts.

Obviously the builders of the tower must have been aware of the creator(s) but quite clearly took them for 'angels' or divine representatives of the Lord, and were quite comfortable about it, but they knew they were 'up above' and calculated that if they built the tower high enough, it would surely increase their chances of encountering them.

As the story in Genesis continues it involves the Lord actually coming down for a good look at what was going on, then returning aloft to report back to the group 'above'. Who were this group? Were they 'angels'? If so, why did not the Lord send one of them 'down' and have him report back to the lord? And so the Lord states to the group "Behold, the people are one; and they have all one language" (would not a divine Lord already be aware of this?).... "And this they begin to do, and now nothing will be restrained from them, which they have imagined to do". This, clearly means, 'if we let them get away with this, they will think that they can do whatever they like – what will they do next?' The Lord continues "go to, let us go down and confound their language, that they may not understand one another's speech". This final going down with their obviously extremely developed telepathic powers and subsequent mental insertions into the minds of the builders, did the trick and the building work came to a halt, with the builders all speaking 'in tongues' (in short 'babbling', which no doubt, is the source of the word 'babbling'). One could imagine the mirth that would be evident among the 'Lord' and his group as they observed the scene below them. Would this seemingly malicious streak be a manifestation of a divine Lord? Surely a commanding authoritative voice accompanied by a good crack or two of thunder would have put a stop to it all quite adequately enough. Apart from having a bit of malicious fun, in this particular case at the expense of their 'creations', the 'creators', in a few cases in the Bible, show an apparent vulnerability, even fear of the human masses and what they might do. Another trait one would not expect in a divine creator. This is particularly evident in Exodus with regard to their, could we say, 'base' on the top of Mount Sinai?

Further to this, one would think that with the centuries of observing and involving themselves with their creations from the 'aliens of Abraham' down through the centuries to Moses' days where the Hebrews were camped at the foot of Sinai, the creator(s) would be well used to the behaviour patterns and predictability of their creations. And so, whether we assign the term 'aliens' or 'angels' to the beings (if we give any credence to the Bible at all) that moved amongst humanity in those days, one thing emerges from it all, and that is, that although the scientists assure us of an interesting future, the present seems positively dull compared to what was going on in the past. Whereas this work looks primarily at the Bible and its events concerning 'angels'(the interpretation the Christian orientated teachings have decided to assign to their close encounters) perhaps it will be necessary to look sometime, at all the other earthly legends some of which are much older in the events spoken of in them, than the biblical happenings, if only to see what the 'aliens' or 'angels' were up to before their involvement in the Mesopotamian area commencing with the motivation (who could have been their possible hybrid creation) of Abraham.

Abraham appears later than 2,000 BC. A lot of centuries had gone by on Earth (but perhaps not for our hypothetical alien creators) since the original creation programme, and the orders to their creations to 'subdue', replenish and till the Earth with the sweat of your brow' had gone out long ago. By now (that is, the appearance of Abraham), many kings, despots, wise rulers, tyrants and potentates had come and gone, all presumably observed and, in some cases, perhaps 'directed' by the creator(s). If, however, we fall back on our old friends 'time dilation', the creator(s) (now assumed, of course, as 'alien') could return when a very long time had passed for those here on Earth, and have rather a lot of catching up to do with regard to how their creations were developing. They may be startled to find that the original creation zone developing so rapidly under the guidance of their chosen created ones, had totally except for a few islands that were the mountain tops), disappeared into the sea, other startling revelations might be the strange, almost planet sized Moon now orbiting this world, and the new earthly angle of axis. Their Earth charts are now useless, an entire remapping of the Earth now, clearly is, necessary. Islands have appeared and disappeared, continental coasts and water lines where different continental drift and subsequent volcanic activity is now much more pronounced. There is much to oversee and to do. They need representatives on Earth, tuned telepathically to their control and to do their bidding without question. They must be 'hybrid creations', born of earthly females and acceptable in the sight of earthlings, but without their savage traits that seem so slow to be consumed by the creator's original bequest of positive and highly advanced genetic material so long ago.

Fairy tale or fact? Who is to say? Were the Patriarchs somehow 'produced', selected for high pursuits? Was the same process used nearly 2,000 years after Abraham to produce the 'Emissary Jesus'? What this process brought about by the insemination of selected females? Were those who postulated, perhaps tongue in check that Jesus was an astronaut, closer to the truth than they thought? Was the prime mission of Jesus to firstly, gather a following by impressive power, select his 'directors' in the Apostles, then become a firm director, or teacher, of righteousness, to the now prolific masses of created entities, to steer their minds away from negative pastime towards positive achievements.

When Jesus said, "What I can do, ye also can do". Apart from all the stage managed illusions, who could really turn water into wine, walk on water or bring back the dead? Was Jesus serious? He did say "ye also can do", and not 'one day' ye will do. Was be implying that the special powers are already in us all? And only need to develop and flower into being? Many earth people with all those gifts and special traits that manifest themselves from time to time in child prodigies and geniuses, may be those that are just a little bit ahead of the rest of us, and all we need is time. Is this the reason for the long and patient observation and 'overseeing', coupled with the occasional abduction for some kind of monitoring or analysis?

Certainly human telepathic powers are showing indications of coming into being. Almost everyone who appears to be on the same 'wavelength' as another who is a wife, husband, friend, partner or whatever, has begun to say something at the same time and on the same topic as the other, or thought of something and the other has said it. They cannot all be coincidences and science has been looking into these and other possibilities, all labelled as paranormal, for quite a few years (certainly in the USSR).

Abraham lived his life up to his 'calling' rather like a sleeper agent and went, when summoned, without question. Could this be due to the implanting of subservient genes to ensure that he did so? It has been assumed by some people that the entire books of Genesis I and II by the Hebrew Moses, were specially written, not only to emphasise their god given right to their promised land (no matter who lived there), but to highlight the Hebrew race as the 'chosen people'. However, other races of the world have made this claim and many other creation stories and myths exist as well as the Christian version, and many come very close to what is inferred in this work, and that is that their ancestors were 'made' by 'sky people'.

From the days when people were consigned to the flames as heretics for daring to even whisper against established beliefs, we hadn't moved forward very far in our 'age of enlightenment' in the totalitarian days of Hitler's Germany, or the former USSR, where people were just as quickly consigned to lunatic asylums for preaching democracy, or concentration camps for political beliefs.

If one had a Catholic upbringing the guilt was so strong, if one had missed church on a Sunday morning for whatever reason, one would walk the other way afterwards if encountering the priest who may have taken the service. One felt sure, in spite of the packed churches, that he would *know*. I can recall stories from my grandparents, both brought up in Ireland, of priests actually taking a cane to youngsters who, in their view, were diverting from the straight and narrow and needed to have the devil beaten out of them. Well, we have made some progress and even over three decades ago, writers felt they could postulate for example, 'was God an astronaut' without feeling the need to take out additional fire insurance.

My own point of view, for what it is worth, is that I would wish every word in the New Testament to be true. There is no better doctrine that includes forgiveness in its policies, rather than putting a contract out on people who may voice opposition to their dogmas. Therefore, the aim throughout this work is simply to reflect on the possible alternative explanations, offered by others before me who could read into strange biblical events, with the benefit of twentieth century technology, a different meaning altogether than that accepted for centuries before the advent of such technology. These suppositions today are not really so fantasy-prone as they may have been viewed by people initially reading the early written 'versions of assertions', decades of further advancement have simply made such postulations even more feasible and acceptable. It is quite obvious that certain events related to in the Bible (and other legends) impressed the ancients greatly to ensure that all the data on such happenings was meticulously recorded for the future generations, and certain 'divine' occurrences, such as the miracles and the appearance of 'angels' would be in that category. Events in eastern legends of the Hindus, Sanskrit references and occurrences of quite an astounding nature in the Mahabharata, make alternative suggestions for angels and pillars of fire pale into insignificance with 'Vimanas' flying about, soaring into the sky with a great roar and climbing to a great height until 'likened to a pearl held at arm's length'. Stories of such dramatic warfare once viewed as fable, now look decidedly like nuclear combat.

Mystical happenings certainly seem to have been occurring in the ancient east that we cannot fathom and they remain that way, with no alternative explanations forthcoming. What alternative could we read into a fiery lance that exploded with the light of 'a thousand suns', an almost exact description of a nuclear explosion. These old historic tales remained mythical for centuries, but the moment the first nuclear weapon was detonated they changed from fable to possibility. In fact, Robert Oppenheimer, one of the scientists on the Manhattan project, quoted from the ancient Indian text "I am become death the destroyer of worlds", when he viewed the awesome nuclear potential.

However, as previously said, whichever way we choose to interpret the actions of all those 'angels' there certainly is a noticeable and distinct absence of them today (at least openly) involving themselves in human affairs, in comparison to their forceful and determined actions in biblical times, and this obviously applied whether they were 'angels' or 'aliens'. The most likely conclusions from this are, they were all 'concoctions', or they have all gone away. The first conclusion, due to the aforesaid abundance of events with celestial or cosmic overtones in other legends, make this most unlikely.

As for them having gone away, we hear of claims of people having actually been removed from the Earth and taken to their craft, and the complete absence of dialogue, except for a slight buzzing noise (which may be the last vestiges of speech), the powers of telepathic influence and communication seem quite strong. The perpetrators use these powers in subduing their victims and for two-way dialogue later, in the cases where the victims attempt communications verbally with their abductors.

In the cases of the mental input that is clearly intended to make their victims forget all about the incident, it would appear that they are not powerful or strong enough to prevent 'mere' humans skilled in the art of hypnotic regression, from gaining access to the mind of the victims and eliciting the dramatic events of their experience from them. Apart from the physical appearance of the abductors to their 'victims', the main purpose of initial 'mind-calming' or telepathic inputs in the victims, is intended to make them more manageable and less traumatised in order to undergo the processes of the abduction peacefully, without panic or struggle.

Later, if the victims of the abduction claims, decide to submit themselves for hypnotic regression sessions, so be it. Perhaps the hypothetical abductors don't really care if their activities are suspected of pondered about, as they may view this as helpful in attuning our minds slowly to the profound possibility and acceptance of their existence, and may assist in some future conclusion, or culmination to it all, which may require their actual appearance to humanity, with the revelation of our true origins.

With regard to the Genesis account for human creation, as much as we may like to believe it all, it could only be accepted by blind faith, and in order to sustain their beliefs, many people modify their viewpoint and make generous concessions to science, whose logic has been eroding away at the original account of human creation for centuries.

As for life on Earth being viewed as a 'mistake' or chance occurrence or accident, and never to be repeated, we would have to concede that the so-called 'big bang' was an accident, that billions of galaxies and exploding suns producing the atoms necessary for everything including the human body form, was as accident and that the many molecular groups constantly being detected in space looking for a suitable home, are also an accident and the billions of galaxies and suns have no planets at all, and our world is the only one in existence, and if they do, they are either gaseous or barren and crater strewn and totally lacking in atmosphere. The stark possibility exists that this assumption could be true, but there appears to be far too much design to the universe making it easy to accept that creation was due to divine command. 'Let there be light', and the command to 'go forth and multiply' really means 'go forth (into

PILLARS OF FIRE

deep space, find suitable worlds, terraform them, colonise them) and multiply', and this would surely (if we survive our own actions) come to pass. It is the way that Genesis relates it that makes it hard to accept. The more likely option is that during the preceding (possible) 16 billion years before the solar system was a 'twinkle in the galactic eye' other world entities had already 'gone forth and multiplied'. Consider how many times the period for human evolution could have occurred during the time the Earth has been suitable for human occupation, and the hugely lengthy dinosaur era.

CHAPTER III

THE 'ANGELS' OF ABRAHAM

The Patriarch Abraham, features highly in our analysis and attempts to identify and interpret the real purpose and agenda of the Messenger' AKA 'Angels' or quite possibly Extra Terrestrials. These beings themselves must have been under the control of a higher authority, who would have been directing their actions from a place 'Not of this Earth', and would have taken their orders from that body.

Unlike modern day humans, who have 'built in' aggression and proclivity for reactive force, even war, when decreed as necessary, the angels knew they could control and direct with impunity, for they had already experienced adulation and awe among Humanity, who worshipped them as messengers from 'Heaven' which was quite natural since they descended and ascended from the sky.

Around 2,000 BC, Abraham was born in Ur Mesopotamia and could be described as the Father of Islam, Judaism and Christianity. His original name was Abram, said to mean 'Exalted Father' but those on high gave him a new name Abraham meaning father of many.

When he received his instructions to leave his home city he was quite aged in our terms and his wife Sarah was in her eighties, Abraham lives for some seventy-five more years left to him after leaving Ur. These ages may seem lengthy to us but are quite short life spans in comparison to the earlier Patriarchs such as Methusala, Lamech, (Noah's father) and Noah himself said to have lived for almost nine hundred years.

When Abraham was 'selected' out or brought under the control of the Angels, he reacted like (in modern parlance) 'a sleeper agent' awaiting the call to action. When the controlling command came 'it stated' "Get thee from thy father's house and travel to a land which I will show thee" (Canaan, later Israel). He obeyed without question. The scriptures do not say how old his father was at this time but to be still living in his father's house at around 100 years of age, seems strange. Sarah, Abraham's wife, must have been living with 'the in laws' at the time. Sarah, in fact, was barren but this would pose no problem for the Angels, as they had the ability to inseminate earthly women barren or not, married or not, as will be shown later with regard to Sampson's mother and of course Mary, the mother of Jesus.

PILLARS OF FIRE

If Abraham was not pre-selected and mentally conditioned to obey, one would have expected him to react quite differently. At first shock, then a string of enquiring questions and a reluctance to leave his established routine but this did not occur. A person not under mental control, would have reacted quite differently with perhaps "Wait a minute, who are you, why me? I have lots to do here, can't you get somebody else". This did not happen and together with his wife and close relatives, he duly departed taking his herds and flocks along with him.

Later, his controllers decided to test his subservience and obedience in an extreme and if he passed this test, they would know that they did have full control of him. He was commanded to sacrifice his son Isaac. He would have complied with this extremely harsh request, and clearly the 'Angels' sensed this and stopped him before he could carry out the order. It was, it would seem, not an act of compassion felt by the Angels, to prevent this senseless killing, as the Angels, as will be shown in the chapter dealing with Moses and the Exodus Saga, had no qualms about destroying the first born among the Egyptians and ordering, during the Desert Wanderings of the Israelites in the wilderness. "Let not a creature that breathes to live, man woman or child" in a coming battle.

There are possibly two reasons why the 'Angels' halted the action of Abraham. Firstly they had proved their point, regarding his obvious obedience and the killing of the child would serve no further purpose, and secondly, they would not wish to appear indebted to Abraham and have him believe he would think the 'Angels' owed him a favour' to be asked for later, which may not suit their purpose.

Isaac would not be the only son Abraham would sire but before his birth, as said, Abraham's wife was barren. When the 'Angels' informed her she would have a child, she must have thought that the Angels were not as clever and knowledgeable as they seemed to think they were, Sarah was quite amused by this information regarding a birth to come, and showed this amusement to the Angel, who surprisingly acted rather petulantly to Sarah's explanation that she was barren by stating "Is anything too difficult for The Lord?"

The Old Testament of course, is based on much older Jewish texts such as The Talmud and so forth, and an interesting story regarding Abraham appears. The Angels of course were always there, it would seem that Abraham in his younger days was something of a warrior. It relates that Abraham, in a certain conflict with King Nimrod, was captured and sentenced to be burned at the stake. But lo! The Angels appear on the scene, flying around and putting out the fire. Clearly Abraham was under their control for quite some time before he was ordered to begin his mission.

PILLARS OF FIRE

Accounts such as these seem hardly credible but so do many other actions involving the Angels still to come, that will be related herein, taken from the Scriptures. The factor of embellishment and exaggeration must be considered over the years, before being set down in the Texts, with perhaps just a kernel of truth in them.

The Old Testament rarely, if ever, mentions Angels equipped with wings but the Patriarchs knew that they ascended and descended from above, which would of course require some sort of power source. "Pillars of Fire" was often mentioned as the power that accomplished their rising up from and descending to Earth. The Ancients being in awe of the power of the Angels, frequently tried to please them. The term 'burnt offering' is often used throughout biblical texts and was commonplace in those times.

The term 'burnt' seems strange as no-one, especially an Angel would want to eat burnt food, it no doubt just meant cooked or perhaps fried over a fire that was obviously burning.

One account in the biblical texts has a certain character, obviously conversing in a 'close encounter' with an Angel, offering food, still described as a 'burnt offering' to an Angel (roast lamb perhaps). The Angel seemed disdainful and unimpressed and stated "Place the offering upon this rock". Then the Angel pointed a special instrument or rod at the offering and "consumed it in a flame". The Angel then rose up in a pillar of flame, obviously with some sort of power pack or device attached to its body. The assumption, of course, by the earthly Observers, was the Angels were rising up to 'Heaven' rather than, perhaps to a waiting craft.

Within the biblical texts the Angels quite often did partake of human food, with no detriment to themselves, and certainly with Abraham and his nephew, Lot, and of course his family, Lot had a wife and two daughters.

As long as the Patriarchs and the masses thought of the zone above the fleecy clouds as 'Heaven' and not outer space, the Angels were more than happy with this and did not fear any challenge to their operations or their physical bodies, which clearly they did possess. But they were vulnerable. In logical and earthly terms, the Angels, after ascending under power, must eventually arrive at some platform, or more likely a structured craft or interplanetary vehicle, which would be obvious to those viewing the Angels 'Rising up!' If not disguised in some fashion, perhaps within a purposely induced 'Cloud'.

They frankly admitted this method of disguising their craft, when stating their forthcoming arrival in Exodus. The expression used by "The Controller" and the crew of Angels to Moses, was clear, when informing him of the (soon to occur) arrival of their craft on Mount Sinai, whereas Moses would attend his forty day instructional course in the spaceship. "I come to thee in a thick cloud", clearly, this 'cloud' that disguised their craft must have been purposely induced, as it must have obviously moved with the craft. A natural cloud would only move with the wind and would only be useful to hide in, but not to move about.

The Angels, in appearance, must have been acceptable to the Patriarchs but, perhaps the actual 'Other World' creatures within their craft may not have been, and their presence would perhaps not be so acceptable, particularly if they resemble the modern day descriptions of the beings observed in 'close encounter' allegations. These are commonly known as 'Greys' with large heads, eyes and spindly arms and legs. They would certainly not have humans prostrating themselves in worship and be admired; they would cause fear, resentment and anger, and, with the typical reaction of humans to destroy that which they fear and don't understand would be apparent. The possibility exists that two types of alien being exist and operate alongside each other. This seems to have been the case in the Travis Walton abduction claim, when, as a forestry worker in the seventies, was abducted for some time into an alien craft. He observed the two types of entities mentioned. In any event, the entities that arrived on Earth in pre-Genesis days, and stated "Let us make men in our image" would certainly not fit the description of the 'Greys'.

If many of the Alien visitors, we have chosen to describe as 'Angels', were so familiar with Earth, they would be extremely familiar with earthly languages, custom foodstuffs and even earthly bacteria and disease but did not fear any risk of contagion in the frequent close encounters.

When mentioning their vulnerability, as any living creature has it would appear the 'Angels' lack any physical strength. An amazing account, involving [2] Abraham's grandson Jacob is related in The Old Testament. In this event, Jacob was having a friendly physical tussle with an 'Angel' he was getting the better of his opponent. The Angel was getting concerned, not by the fact that he was losing the contest, but the Entity has observed that daylight was fast approaching and this seemed to bother the 'Angel' who didn't seem to want to be seen in broad daylight. However, Jacob would not let go until the Angel 'Blessed' him.

Jacob is also well known for his observation of a group of Angels, ascending and descending on some type of escalator, described as a 'ladder' meaning of course that the craft that obviously existed must have been very low, as the 'Angels' had no need for their jet pack equipment. There must have been a very low cloud base or Jacob would have observed the craft and we would have another account similar to Ezekiel when struggling to describe his craft and its occupants, who, incidentally, took no precautions with regard to disguising themselves in a 'cloud'.

Abraham has many adventures throughout Mesopotamia, even into Egypt, along with the so-called 'Fertile Crescent'. But it was in Canaan that the 'Angels' made clear to him that this would be the Promised Land.

All this time, Abraham was travelling with his ever increasing herds and flocks. The same of course applied to his nephew, Lot. They also were described as having servants, so together with the two families and all their accoutrements, they must have been a formidable group when pitching up to rest, feed and sleep, and covered an extensive area. At this point there was a famine in the land and they were heading towards Egypt to find food, so goes the script, but with all that cattle and sheep they certainly should not have been short of meat.

Abraham's wife Sarah was said to have been quite attractive. Abraham worried about this, as The Pharaoh, ever on the lookout for more attractive females for his Harem, may have had Abraham killed. So, on a couple of occasions Abraham passed Sarah off as his sister. In an old mature leather-bound copy of The Old Testament, obtained from my local library, I read an account, where two beings visited The Pharaoh in his sleep, they frightened him greatly, which implies that these visitors were the previously described 'Greys' and not the Angels that were familiar to Moses, Abraham and others. If so, in his dreams he would simply have shouted for his guards to have them killed. The message they transmitted to The Pharaoh was that Sarah was Abraham's wife and not his sister, and that he should keep his hands off her. They also made him aware that Abraham was under their control.

A couple of angels landed close to Abraham's tent and he ran to meet them. Running for a man of over a hundred years old, is quite an achievement by anyone's standards. He welcomes them into his tent for the formal hospitality of those times for the obligatory food and drink. These 'Angels' are the beings or messengers that informed Sarah although barren, that she would have a son.

After the hospitalities, one of the 'Angels' outlines their mission, regarding the depravity of the cities of Sodom and Gomorrah. Obviously they had been 'informed' perhaps by Abraham but, after all his nephew Lot did live in the Gate and would be, by now, fully aware of the sordid practices of the occupants and would surely have discussed this issue with Abraham. The 'Angels' were also aware of the abhorrent nature of the population and made it clear they came 'down' (from where?) to investigate the 'reports', "To see if the outcry that has come to me is as bad as I have heard". On the religious side of this issue, if a divine God and His 'Angels' were present, rather than extra-terrestrial, under control of a different nature, then, as we are taught that God knows and sees all, He would already know what was happening in these cities and no-one would need to 'come down' to verify the reports. Other indications are apparent, pointing towards Abraham being the reporter (after all, he was in frequent communication with the 'Angels') such as his anxiety when learning of the dire consequences to come, that would be metered out to the depraved occupants of the cities. It was at this point that Abraham, perhaps feeling a little guilty, began his bargaining process, regarding any righteous persons that may exist within the population. At first the figure was 50, which seemed a tall order as the 'Angels' (one of which had already moved among the population), were confident that figure would never be realised.

It seems fairly certain that the 'Angels' were quite confident that 'D' day [for destruction] would not be prevented and no doubt had already formulated and put their plans in place. It soon became clear to Abraham that he had failed in his efforts to save anyone. Two of his Angelic visitors, then broke off and travelled to the gate of the City, to inform Lot and his family of the fate soon to befall the cities and that they should make preparations to leave the area first thing in the morning.

Again, more hearty eating and drinking at Lot's hospitality and they began to settle down for the night. Unknown to them, the arrival of the 'Angels' must have been spotted and the news quickly spread among the population.

The occupants of the city, ever on the lookout for 'new blood' decided to look into this for themselves. Consequently, the depraved mob showed up at Lot's house in the Gate. No mob can approach quietly, and Lot appeared, demanding to know what it was all about. The ringleaders made it clear that they wished to 'know' the visitors and that he should bring them out immediately. The phrase 'to know' is often used in the scriptures "And Adam 'knew' his wife Eve". This was biblical parlance for sexual activity.

At this point, Lot begins to panic, he even offers his own daughters to them, if they would just leave the 'Angels' alone. Whether the mob had already 'known' Lot's daughters, is not clear but later, it will be shown that His daughters were quite capable of the kind of behaviour that had gained the city its reputation in the first place.

However, Lot's offer did not appease the mob and as a result, they began to push past Lot to get at the 'Angels', but they had been aware of the commotion outside and were quite ready to deal with any situation that arose.

PILLARS OF FIRE

The 'Angels' then appeared and with some kind of weapon they were equipped with, used it to blind the ringleaders of the crowd. The lustful mob, then rapidly began to disperse. They may have been blind drunk but did not wish to be blind permanently.

At this point, the 'Angels' thought it desirable to hasten the plan of departure and fully briefed Lot and his family of the events soon to come to pass.

Plainly, nuclear annihilation from above. The 'Cities of the Plain', Sodom and Gomorrah were to be totally destroyed.

It is obviously quite clear now that these entities we call 'Angels' are extra-terrestrial operatives, who, along with their previous generations, had been evolving themselves in the affairs of humanity ever since the initial 'creators' of long ago.

Lot, now fully appreciates the urgent need for rapid departure but still takes time out to warn certain others close to him and his family (presumably righteous) that may have resided, not in, but in close proximity to the city. They don't believe him as his story seems preposterous.

The 'Angels' then direct Lot on the route he must take, not only to avoid the (nuclear) blast but also the fallout. At this point they make it absolutely clear that they must keep going forward and not to look back, which of course Lot's wife does, and in the well known story turns to a 'Pillar of Salt'.

The curious geology of the area some archaeologists and biblical investigators accept as the likely place where these events took place, does show salt pillars, hard crusty effigies, some sculptured by the wind that look like human figures. Lot and his daughters experience the flash, blasts and dust blowing behind them and resist looking back and struggle on, eventually to reach the sanctuary of a cave in the mountains, overlooking the Plain. When things begin to settle down and they take stock of their situation, a curious event of an incestuous nature takes place.

Lots daughters, not having married, for obvious reasons regarding the suitability of the depraved cities men-folk, became concerned that Lot will have no son and heirs, and conspire to get their father drunk on wine.

Lot's daughters then both have sex with him. Since these people were deemed to be among the 'Righteous', it may indicate the depths of depravity that the other city dwellers had sunk to. It came to pass, that both daughters became pregnant and gave birth to sons, the scriptures name as 'Moab' and 'Benn-Ami'.

PILLARS OF FIRE

During the afore-mentioned destruction of the Cities of the Plain, Abraham stood on a high safe plateau alongside one of the 'Angels' who had interacted with him during this process of destruction. It was described as "Rising as smoke from a Furnace", clearly a mushroom cloud from the detonation. Curiously, no mention is made of masses of casualties in the aftermath. No weeping and wailing and 'gnashing of teeth' promises of repentance and so-forth. Everything just ceased to exist. It is was a nuclear blast and some investigators of the suspected area have discovered vitrified rocks and fused green glass, seemingly verifying the signature of a nuclear event, then comparisons could be made with the similar fused green glass (i.e. sand) found at the nuclear test site in New Mexico and it was the same.

Abraham, now aged and weary of his life's experiences, passes away at the age of 175 years. However, all the conditions had been met since his instruction to 'get thee from thy father's house'. All the descendants, marriages and plans set for the future generations were in place and moving towards the final goal (the Promised Land).

CHAPTER IV

THE ANGELS OF EXODUS

The story of Moses and his encounters with the mysterious entities we know as 'Angels', are just as prolific and mysterious as those who interacted with Abraham. Although Abraham had 'set the ball rolling' so to say, things did not always go to plan. The Israelites are in slavery in Egypt and their numbers are naturally increasing. At this point, Moses enters the frame.

The Pharaoh is worried about this population explosion occurring among the Hebrews and any troublesome future arising, and orders that all the newborn male children be killed. This would not be the last horrific action of this type. It would prevail up to the time of Herod and The New Testament when he heard of a Messiah or possible King of the Jews had been born. The well known story [1] of Moses placed in his reed basket to avoid the "Slaughter of the Innocents" now begins.

Moses thrives and grows up alongside the future Pharaoh Ramses the second as half brother. He would have received the best possible education and had access to the Great Libraries and the long history of the Egyptian dynasties and also the chequered history of his own people, the Hebrews and Israelites with their 'Promised Land' beliefs. However, it doesn't seem clear when Moses realises his own Hebrew beginnings.

Moses was observed and then rescued from the Nile by the Pharaoh's daughter no less. She named him 'Moses'. This name is said to mean in the Egyptian language 'Begotten of' but in Hebrew 'To draw out'. It must be said, that this babe in the basket story was not unique and may have been influenced by an earlier event where the future King Sargon of Mesopotamia was rescued from the Euphrates as a babe in a basket.

Moses, during his growth and maturity to manhood, notices the cruelty of the slave masters, when deciding a slave may not be seen as performing well, or strenuously enough and was duly whipped. At one point, with great detriment to himself, he intervenes and kills one of the sadistic punishers. His own punishment for this, no doubt influenced heavily by his half brother Ramses, was to be exiled into The Wilderness [3] eventually to Midian.

It seems clear that the 'Controllers' had been very much involved in 'pre-selecting' Moses, for reasons best known to themselves, in order to fit in with their plans and may even have influenced his survival by mental insertion, thereby ensuring his mother saved him from the afore-mentioned 'slaughter of innocents'. However, the 'Angels' were ready and waiting for him' when he arrived in Midian.

Moses now begins his series of encounters with his future controllers, that we know as the 'Angels'.

At one point, during his newly established way of life, the 'Angels' decided, that the time was right to implement their plans for Moses and 'Operation Exodus', which he had been chosen to lead by a shining craft descending behind what the Scriptures describe as a 'Bush', clearly it must have been a large copse, big enough to hide the outline of the craft. It must have been on a well-worn route, used by Moses for them to choose this location.

Moses duly appears [4] he is puzzled, yet intrigued by this unusual encounter, observing a glittering effect of the foliage moving in the breeze, that gave the impression of burning.

Startled, but nevertheless curious, he made to approach it for closer inspection. He is stopped when a voice tells him to "Go no further" and to ensure he did not, the voice commands him to remove his sandals. Anyone who tries to walk on the burning sand of the Middle East or any country with a hot climate barefoot, knows it's quite impossible. Moses must have moved the top sand away before removing his sandals, in order to stand in the cooler earth beneath. Moses is now informed of his objective and that he has been chosen to lead his people out of bondage. Moses is shocked and not a little nervous and starts to find reasons to get out of his assignment. Again, as in the story of Abraham, his reaction is devoid of any questioning or enquiry, as to who was communicating with him and where they are from and so forth. It is as though he sensed that he would have to do something profound, but tried his best to get out of it.

He starts by saying that 'His people would not believe him and not regard him as anyone special'. He also adds, "I am heavy of mouth and tongue". But the controller assures him by stating "I will be thy mouth, I will be with thee and give you the words to say". (Clearly, telepathic control). Moses has a staff and by some power source it becomes a powerful weapon. The 'Angel' tells Moses to pass the staff over his hand, which then becomes leprous, after he is told to pass it over again, the wound immediately heals. The staff turns into a snake, he drops it, but quickly regains his confidence and picks it up and it turns back into a staff.

Moses now begins to feel more self assured and confident and believes this power demonstrated to him, will enable him to be successful in his mission and he departs to ready himself to leave Midian and return to confront The Pharaoh in his court.

Moses does not intend to go 'cap in hand' to The Pharaoh but to confidently demand 'Let my people go'. Biblical researches attempt to explain away all the 'miraculous' events that were alleged to have occurred in this Exodus story, even the parting of the Red (Reed?) Sea. Many of them do occur, such as plagues of locusts and so forth, but to have each occurrence happening 'coincidently' as and when required, is stretching coincidence quite considerably.

However, this work is confined to an objective analysis of the identity of these alleged 'Angels' or controllers throughout the Biblical Scriptures, involving so many Patriarchs and the power and miraculous ability given to them. Also, since they are clearly 'not of this earth', there is no other title for them than 'Extra Terrestrial'.

Moses, together with his brother Aaron, sets off to fulfil his mission, confident and determined to succeed. We must comment, that when Moses was conversing with the 'voice' in what he perceived as a 'burning bush', that he did not mention the fact, that he was banished from Egypt and the reason why. When Moses was making excuses for not returning that ought to have been the primary excuse, as his life would obviously be in danger.

This factor would certainly be on his mind as he journeyed back to Egypt. Would he be immediately arrested and put to death? But his confidence and self-assuredness was at its peak, instilled in him by the obvious mental and telepathic power of his controlling 'Angel' at the 'close encounter' in Midian. On arrival, the first thing he does is to assure his people that he intends to free them from bondage and explains his encounter and new-found power and that he intends to confront The Pharaoh. And so, Moses enters the Palace and meets The Pharaoh face to face. He states his purpose and that 'God' has given him the power to achieve it at all cost.

The Pharaoh's initial reaction, one would have thought, would be to have his soldiers arrest Moses and put him to death, but he was probably aware that he had contacted his people. The old fear of a rebellious uprising would be on his mind.

Nevertheless, the Pharaoh reacts angrily and roars at Moses "We know nothing of your God; you have the audacity to tell me to release my workforce". "I will tell you what I will do, I will not only retain them, I will increase their workload".

PILLARS OF FIRE

Moses leaves the court of The Pharaoh, his confidence somewhat diminished. When he confronts his people again, he finds them in an angry mood, they turn on Moses, and make it clear that they wish he had stayed in Midian and not made this bid to release them. This was the first of many complaints to Moses during the following stages of Exodus. In any case some of them were reluctant to leave and travel into The Wilderness and an uncertain future but the longing for their promised land was always with them.

Moses and Aaron are at a loss as to what they would do next. In some way, not made clear in the Biblical account, Moses contacts his controller for advice. Clearly, he must have been informed of the 'procedure' during his Midian encounter. Moses is told that they are just part of the overall plan and that everything is proceeding as planned and is on schedule and that he should approach The Pharaoh, confidence boosted and to demonstrate the power given to him, He returns, The Pharaoh still stubbornly refuses to allow the (Israelites) Hebrews to leave. It is then that Moses demonstrates his power.

He calls down fire from above, clearly assisted by the Controllers; he inflicts the Egyptians with plague, frogs, gnats, flies boils, huge hailstones, locusts, darkness over the land. The Nile turns to blood. Most horrific of all, this time it was The Egyptian first born who were to die, by what The Bible describes as a 'Destroying Angel' [6]. If this really happened, it demonstrates how far-removed these 'Angels' were from anything 'divine' or 'holy' or emissaries of a loving God. Furthermore, this ruthlessness would be demonstrated often, during his long desert trek.

During the tenth plague [7] the phrase known as 'The Passover' occurs. The Destroying 'Angel' passes over the houses of The Israelites, the Slaughtering 'Angel', clearly, in some aerial craft, equipped with the technology to see into the houses and destroy the newborn babes.

The Pharaoh's son, though not a babe, is also killed. In preparation for this event, the Israelites were told to paint distinctive crosses on their houses. Obviously the aerial craft had no problem seeing into the houses; it had only to ensure it was hitting the right ones.

Strangely, the mass-murder of innocent children is remembered as something to celebrate. This callous act, and others still to come, are specifically directed by the 'Angels' when they are told before a battle, "Let not any creature that breathes to live". Finally, The Pharaoh's resolve is broken and he tells Moses and Aaron to get out of Egypt immediately.

Now the Great Trek begins [8] over a million people with all their accoutrements and possessions begin trooping out into the Wilderness.

PILLARS OF FIRE

Even then, some were reluctant to go, although they knew they had no choice, for most certainly, the Pharaoh would take his revenge on them, knowing that Moses with his new found powers had left, so they were in a classic 'catch 22' situation.

The fact was, although in bondage, they had grown used to their Egyptian lifestyle, they lived in relative safety and were paid in kind, with wheat, beer and other foodstuffs. But now they had to keep themselves focused on the fact that they were fulfilling the dream of heading to 'the promised land' but, they had no idea just how long it would take to achieve this aim.

As things slowly returned to some semblance of normality in Egypt after the ten plagues, The Pharaoh's anger had slowly increased and reached boiling point-, when dwelling on what had happened, especially, the death of his own son. He began contemplating on revenge. He knew that the tracks the mass of people had left in their wake, even after a couple of sandstorms, would still be discernible and easy to follow.

The Pharaoh decided that the time was right to send his formidable army to pursue and annihilate them. He would not go, but he would instruct his commanders that the Israelites would probably have to cross The Red Sea at some point, and time it to catch them with the sea at their backs.

As The Pharaoh did stay behind to live on, it most likely was Ramses Π, who was alleged to be The Pharaoh during this event. The Bible mentions that The Pharaoh's heart was 'hardened' before making the decision to follow Moses and the Israelites. If the 'Angels' did have these strong telepathic powers as portrayed in the actions of Moses, then it is quite possible that it was the 'Angels' who planted the idea into the mind of The Pharaoh and it was 'they who hardened his heart'. Of course, the 'Angels' knew the plan that was to follow and it would suit their purpose to lure The Pharaoh's army into a situation where they (the 'Angels') could eliminate them.

And so it came to pass, that the pursing army did catch up with the Israelites as intended. When The Israelites had reached the intended point of crossing the sea, they heard the thunder of hooves and saw the dust clouds rising. They began to wail and cry out in fear but Moses calms them and tells them to fear not and to "Watch the power invested in me". At this point, he demonstrates the incredible power in his 'staff'. As he faces the waters he raises it above his head and lo! The waters divide and pile up on each side and in their parting, leave a dry strip and The Israelites move rapidly across the river. Having witnessed this amazing event and the power evident in their leader, it is strange that so much wailing and complaining continued during the period after their crossing, over far less serious issues than a pursuing army attempting to destroy them. The 'Angels' now begin to implement their pre-planned operation. An aerial craft could be the only explanation for what happened next.

The Commander of the pursing Egyptian army must have witnessed the amazing event of the parted waters and The Israelites hurrying across and flinched a little at this fantastic show of power wielded by their leader.

The 'Angels' now ably assisting The Hebrews, moved into the tactical position to slow the advance of The Egyptians, Exodus clearly states (it could only be a laser beam) The 'Angels' sliced off the wheels of the chariots. "That they 'Drave' then heavily". Clearly this was done from above.

However, the 'Angels' could only deal with the leading chariots and others strangely, continued the pursuit. Even the most incompetent of commanders, one would have thought, would not lead his army into such an obvious trap but perhaps they were more afraid of The Pharaoh's punishment, if they abandoned the pursuit and returned to Egypt with their mission unaccomplished.

At this point, the last of the Hebrews had reached the other side and Moses once more raised his staff and lo! The waters fell upon them and the entire pursing army was drowned. This would have been a major event in Egyptian history and researchers of the Egyptian dynasties have pointed out that their priests and scribes recorded all events, even what could be described as trivia such as the passing of migratory birds but they also reveal, that some Pharaohs, wishing to claim the glory of past events, obliterated the cartouche of the preceding Pharaoh and added their own symbol.

With this kind of arrogance and self-importance, it is entirely possible that the current Pharaoh (Ramses II)? Forbade any mention of his army's pursuit and failure on pain of death. An entire army with full weaponry, defeated by unarmed former slaves in open country? He would never retain his power with such shame He would become a laughing stock of the future in Egyptian annals.

As time passed, Moses and his followers, no doubt mentally influenced by his controller, were heading to a place well familiar to Moses, Midian.

This place appears to be one of the 'Angels' command posts, as it was here, that Moses received his assignment and would also be the place where Moses would be instructed over a lengthy period and given his code of behaviour patterns, that the Hebrews and their future generations must follow. They had arrived at the base of Mt Sinai.

The next happening was most certainly an extra-terrestrial event. Moses was made aware that a craft would arrive and would descend upon the mountain top, but before this could happen, Moses was instructed to 'set bounds' around the 'mount' and take heed that "No man should approach higher" (except Moses of course). Moses was warned that anyone that does so will be killed.

"Whether it be man or beast, it will be killed or 'shot through'!" (Some form of laser weaponry)? Clearly, the occupants of the craft would not be concerned about a goat or a cow observing their craft; it seems to have been a device that would fire automatically, pre-set to do so if any living thing approached it.

Obviously, it was disarmed when Moses approached, or he would have been 'shot through'. He would also have been sworn to secrecy regarding his forty days tutoring session, where he was taught how to construct a landing place or 'tabernacle' set far from the crowd, in order that the 'Angels' could descend to converse with Moses and Aaron and to lead them on their journey. He was also tutored in the construction of a formidable weapon which also served as a communication device in order to converse or receive instructions The Ark of the Covenant.

Moses was told "I will come to thee in a thick cloud" and once more warned him about anyone approaching further than the bounds that had been set.

Eventually, an audible rumbling occurred as the craft arrived and descended on the mount, which was "All of a smoke". It's unlikely that this was an exhaust system of the craft but a 'force field' causing the dust to billow up around it. The mountain quaked and rumbled and The Hebrews reeled back 'sore afraid'.

As said, it seems strange that the people experiencing such wonders would continue to complain so easily about any perceived threat and fall back into relaxed indifference, particularly with regard to their behaviour when Moses was up in Mount Sinai receiving his instructions, for some six weeks.

Moses knew that it was time for him to ascend the mount and assigned Aaron, his second in command, to rule. And once more warned about the mortal danger, should any of The Hebrews try to advance further than the bounds that were set.

It is doubtful that Moses knew how long he would be away from his people, as he would have told them, thus preventing the negative behaviour that would occur during his absence, the people [10] had no idea when (or perhaps if) he would return. And so Moses began to trek up the mountain to encounter the 'Angels' face to face, that had concealed themselves from him in the 'Burning Bush' episode. He would be very apprehensive at this point.

PILLARS OF FIRE

The Ten Commandments on the stone slabs, that were the directives for basic civilised behaviour patterns for the people, were described as being cut into the tablets by 'the Finger of God', once more, a laser instrument.

Written in stone is obviously a longer lasting method than any scroll or parchment and they would be placed safely in the Ark, which as will be shown, would be deadly to anyone attempting to capture it, or even touch it, except The Hebrews of course, but even they had to be wary.

Aaron it would appear seemed to have little control over the people during the first few weeks of the absence of Moses [11]. It seems the people had not forgotten their lost 'gods' so easily and began to construct a golden bull (not a calf as stated) but a symbol 'god of power' among others, and not a single God or 'Yahweh' that the Hebrews alone worship, as directed in The Ten Commandments.

In order to construct this large Golden Bull, one wonders where the gold came from; after all, they were supposed to be downtrodden slaves without wealth and only existing by 'kind permission' of the Egyptian slave masters.

At this point Moses had completed his instructional course and began his trek down the mountain with the stone tablets to rejoin his people. When reaching the base, he observes the golden bull and the worship and revelry occurring and throws down the Tablets in a rage. It is stated in the Scripture, that Moses had the effigy ground into dust and sprinkled on water and made the Hebrews drink of it.

Eventually the furore dies down and some semblance of normality ensues. A substantial amount of Biblical text is devoted to the construction of the Tabernacle, to house The Ark of the Covenant.

When the 'Angels' are in the tabernacle, the Hebrews do not go forth but when the 'Angels' ascend back up to their craft, they journey on once more. They had many battles to face before reaching their Promised Land.

The power in the formidable weapon (the Ark) would aid them greatly.

They followed the light beam of the 'Angels' craft by night and the 'Pillar of Cloud' that hid it from the crown when moving forward by day. They could not simply 'Beeline' for 'Palestina' as it was called in the Script, they had to confront opposing forces or go around them.

During their travels Moses did not always see eye to eye with his brother Aaron, and Moses, whose days were numbered, had to appoint a successor.

Like any good commander, Moses appoints spies to go on ahead and evaluate the opposition's numbers, strengths, weaponry, etc., and whether they would be hostile or allow Moses' large numbers to pass by peacefully.

When they carried out this reconnaissance at Canaan, the spies returned with a positive report regarding the land and it's fertility but urges caution, as any attack campaign could end in disaster due to the strength of the enemy forces.

The Israelites have to be continually assured and reminded of all the assistance the 'Angels' have given them, and in any conflict to come, they would ably assist once more. They also knew that news travels fast across the camel routes, and no doubt the stories that had travelled ahead of them, regarding the 'Angels' power and help to acquire past victories, that such stories would, no doubt be embellished and cause fear with each telling.

This may have helped in their previous confrontations, but there was little evidence of this, when they confronted Jericho after crossing the River Jordan, but the power of their Ark is nigh.

As it turned out, Moses would never reach the 'Promised Land' himself and would soon pass away. After forty years travelling and the fact that their objective could actually be seen in the distance must have been a great disappointment for him.

At the time of his farewell address to The Hebrews, their numbers would have greatly increased. With more births than deaths, many of them would have known no other existence than the nomadic life and would have depended on the stories related to them from their parents and The Elders.

At this point, The Israelites are camped on the plains of Moab, just east of the borders of Canaan but another water barrier separated them, which is the Jordan River.

Moses had carried out the bulk of the mission in bringing the Hebrews this far, but he is now 120 years old and decides to hand over command to Joshua. The death of Moses is a mystery in itself, as the Scripture states "His eyes were not dimmed nor his natural force abated", in other words he was not ready for death and no-one knows where his tomb is. This gives rise to the possibility, that the controllers, removed him off the Earth for his just rewards, as Elijah would be, when 'taken up to Heaven in a whirlwind', in full view of his successor Elisha.

A better reward for Moses perhaps, would have been to allow him to reach The Promised Land after all his efforts.

CHAPTER V

WEAPONS FROM THE ANGELS

The Israelites now pledge their allegiance to their new leader Joshua. Having observed the tactics of Moses [1] Joshua sends out spies to assess what would confront them when approaching this great walled city, which seemed impregnable. The crossing of the Jordan River holds no fear for them, as they had little problem crossing the Red Sea, but this time Moses was no longer with them and they wondered if the power within the Rod would still prevail.

However, as it happened, this time the fearsome weapon that had been given to them at Sinai, was about to make its debut, namely The Ark of The Covenant, it contained nothing but the Tablets of the Ten Commandments.

The controllers had supplied new ones to Moses after he had admitted to the controllers of his rage at what had happened on his descent from Sinai.

The scripture uses a strange phrase used by the 'Angel' regarding the lapses and complaining of the Israelites. "They are a stiff-necked people".

The time had come to cross the River Jordan.

The Israelites had been instructed on the following procedure, no doubt from the 'Angels' through Joshua. The Priests would carry The Ark with its staves inserted and the armed Israelites, who could now be called soldiers, would each carry a trumpet. When they approached the river, the same miraculous parting of the waters occurred, when the Ark started to cross with the priests. It is doubtful that the soldiers patrolling the walls of the City, had observed this miraculous event as when the Hebrews arrived, they did not seem fearful, but had they known what was to come, they would (to use a biblical expression) have been 'sore afraid'. The soldiers of the Hebrew army were about to learn of the destructive capabilities of sound, augmented by the power within The Ark and also by the vocal sounds from the many voices and the fearsome vibrating tone of the trumpets.

Everyone knows that jet aircraft are capable of breaking windows, if diving at supersonic speed over a built-up area which happened often when flight testing during the earlier attempts to break the sound barrier. Also, intense operatic singing, at a constant note, has broken many a wine glass.

Another occurrence, less well know, was an event in a French factory.

Workers were reporting sick with nausea and headaches all from around one particular area. The resonance was traced to a certain air conditioning unit.

A sound and acoustic team were called in. They replicated it at a higher tone and frequency aimed at a brick wall and cracks appeared in the brickwork.

Above the city, the soldiers looked down in amusement from the high wall at this strange assembly marching around their city. Seeing the golden container they were carrying, they would have assumed it was treasure to offer to the city fathers, in order to gain entrance to the city and the many trumpeters to entertain them.

The soldiers on the wall must have relaxed and lost interest, as all they observed was this group repetitively walking around their city, as the Hebrews had been instructed to walk around the walls six times each day for six days and on the seventh, to walk around it seven times [3] perhaps this was a plot in order to make the soldiers of the city relax and see them as no threat, or anything to worry about.

However, it was then that they blasted away loudly with their trumpets and the Hebrews "shouted with a great shout". This had the desired effect and the mighty walls cracked and tumbled down, immediately the armed soldiers stormed in and took the city.

Strangely, in their next campaign against a less heavily defended city, called Ai, Joshua's army lost their battle. Having become rather heavily dependent on the controllers, Joshua enquires of them, how they appeared to be abandoned by them. He was told, it was a punishment for the looting of Jericho, gold, silver, jewels and expensive robes, and that it was a 'covenant' violation. (Thou shalt not steal). This is strange, as in previous campaigns they took all the spoils of war, including all the livestock and received no rebuke from the controllers at all.

Joshua eventually takes Canaan and distributes the land among the twelve tribes of The Israelites. [4] Joshua himself eventually stands down after a series of farewell speeches reminding the people to remember the power of the 'Angels' and to make no more lapses in their behaviour. Although during their desert campaigns they frequently refer to the 'Lord' as overseeing all their deeds and rendering such destructive and lethal assistance, it cannot possibly be the 'Lord God' of Christian belief. In reality, they believed that everything they did in battle, with all the killing destroying and smiting their enemies, was attributed to their controllers, the 'Angels'.

PILLARS OF FIRE

We may refer again to the particular event where an 'Angel' instructed them to kill everyone or everything that breathes, men women, children and even their animals as this classified their wealth and position in society.

We may also wish to recall the barbarity of the 'Destroyer' and its craft, killing new born children during the 'Passover'. It is simply not possible to accept that a divine holy 'God' whose own commandment was 'Though shalt not kill', would condone such acts.

This obvious contradiction is unmentioned in the texts. On another occasion on their travels, the Israelites had no part in a slaughter of 150,000 Assyrians when the Hebrews were sleeping and an 'Angel' was totally responsible.

It must be mentioned [p55] that 'Giants' were frequently referred to in the Bible, which is a problem for biblical researchers. They are spoken of in a 'matter of fact' way, however, as we suspect, the 'Angels' are masters of, not only a Genetic Creation, but can easily make barren women pregnant, the invention of huge entities for their own purposes, would not seem impossible. Ancient legends clearly state that 'Gods' from the sky came down and built the huge edifices that exist around the world, in particular South America. The Giants are often portrayed as brutish as, for example, 'Goliath' who was despatched by David and his Slingshot.

The 'Angels' however, could create more intelligent beings with great strength, Sampson for instance, who helped The Israelites greatly, against The Philistines, eliminating the enemy with the Jawbone of an Ass.

The mother of Sampson was impregnated by a descending 'Angel'.

Clearly 'Genetic Creation', as of course was Mary, the Mother of Jesus who had not yet 'known' a man.

Giants in large numbers were mentioned during The Israelites' desert trekking and the returning spies, after encountering them, returned with a fearful story. "We be not able to go up against them, they are a land of Giants, and we are as 'Grasshoppers'" in their sight. The Hebrews avoided this encounter.

The Ark of the Covenant still remained as a powerful weapon for the Israelites and it existed through the centuries after they had reached their Promised Land. When Moses was originally instructed, how to construct it from Gold and a certain type of wood, with precise instructions regarding its dimensions, the secrets of its power may not have been obvious to him, but to modern day scientists or physicists, these secrets may well have been identifiable. The 'controllers' would be safe in the knowledge that Moses would just 'follow orders'.

We have well reached the point where we could accept these 'Angels' as extra-terrestrial beings, since they are not the product of the imaginations of just a few individuals, but occur throughout different periods involving different people. They no doubt live for centuries as humans will eventually do, and may have already done so in antediluvian times, when the extremely long life-spans mentioned so 'matter-of-factly' in Genesis, are attributed to them.

The 'Angels' operating on Earth in Biblical times, during their interactions with The Patriarchs, felt that they could do anything they liked, at anytime, at any place and acted as though humans were their 'property'. Startlingly this may be true in a sense. It has been suggested that the Garden of Eden was an extra-terrestrial genetic creation centre, discarding failures, (evident in the disjointed bone fossil evidence) and finishing with the advanced upright intelligent Cro-Magnon species, endowed with a larger brain than modern day humans. They were artistic, imaginative and creative and seemed to be a successful creation. Nevertheless, it still seemed necessary to destroy humans in large numbers in the days of Noah, as humanity at that time, had degenerated somewhat in their behaviour patterns.

Clearly, the creators, or 'Angels' are still around observing us, evidently in the UFO phenomena, but as said in the early part of this work, they can no longer masquerade as 'Angels' due to the technological advancement of humans, who would no longer fall on their faces in adoration. So now, they kept their distance but still take humans off the Earth from time to time for genetic analysis and development, evident in the many abduction cases.

However, in the abductions, humans are just as helpless in their hands as they ever were. The main point is that there must be a culmination to all of this at some point, when they decide that humanity is ready for such enlightenment but, with the human proclivity for aggression out of fear and our 'shoot first and ask questions later attitude, they would surely not assess the time was right for 'Revelations' of our possible origins. So, a 'low profile' policy is the order of the day.

The decision will finally be made in planet 'Heaven' by the controlling body of beings coursing through our skies all over the world. The important question is, how would humans handle such revelations? In their eyes we must still appear as intelligent savages. Every new invention is assessed for its potential as a weapon by the military. The amazing advancements in our space programme, must be worrisome for these alleged beings and if they are the offspring of the initial creators (i.e. their forebears) they would have a great responsibility for humanity inherited from those times.

If we reverse the situation where humans achieve interstellar, rather than interplanetary, travel as we will one day do so, (E.T. permitting) and we see it as our duty to promote intelligence in creatures struggling to survive, and they advance to the point of entering the cosmic domain yet retained aggressive and warlike tendencies, would we allow them to do so?.

Some alleged 'abductees', report amazing things, such as observing embryos in bluish fluid and reveal under hypnosis, that a massive creative programme is taking place, producing human/ET hybrids (which we ourselves may be) possibly genetically advanced, with positive tendencies eliminating the negative, and to be gradually inserted among current Humanity.

Since abduction claims exist worldwide, these beings could duplicate any racial appearance and must consider their actions as quite straightforward. We may recall the 'Angels' that informed Sarah, Abraham's wife, when told she would have a son, although barren "Is anything too difficult for The Lord?". The 'Angel' seemed surprised she even questioned it.

Although the Genesis account is attributed to Moses by the British and Foreign Bible Society, many others were involved in biblical writings. The Gospels and so forth, all fallible humans, and before the invention of the printing press, many alterations of the texts took place to please various rulers, Emperors and Kings, we cannot be sure what was taken out, altered or added to the texts.

To raise the point of 'contradiction' again, regarding the stern commandments and at the same time, mass slaughter of the newborn, and in the savage battles of The Israelites, the biblical writers conveniently placed the blame on the 'Angels' for directing their actions. Perhaps to ease their own conscience.

There is certainly a great discrepancy in the actions of those times, compared to the teachings of Jesus (suggested by some as a human/ET hybrid) centuries later. His teachings were so profound that if everyone followed them, there would be a perfect world, but noble teachings do not produce noble and perfect humans, who have too many faults and imperfections, which in spite of the great 'culling' of humanity in the days of Noah and The Flood, still remain.

With regard to the aforementioned slaughter in Exodus, the writings are attributed to Moses, a man who, according to some scholars and researchers, never existed. In any case, others would have to finish the story, as Moses died before the saga of Jericho and the Battles before taking Canaan.

Nevertheless, it is difficult to state that the 'Angels' and their interactions with humans never existed or took place, as they are spread through The Bible over all the epochs and involved many people. For example, Solomon, David, Ezekiel, Elijah, Elisha and others. As said, it seems these Patriarchs were very special people, possibly ET hybrids under control of the 'Angels', who, through mental action could 'activate' them as required to do their bidding and to obey, without question, as indicated with Abraham and Moses.

The 'Angels', evident in their initial "Let us 'make' men in our image" were masters of genetic manipulation and reproduction. Even anthropologists when commenting on the disjointed and rather puzzling (and meagre) human bone fossil evidence, when considering the shortcomings of the Darwinian Theory, at least in one case, stated "The fossil evidence for human emergence from simian kind, seems more like the result of an 'experiment' than a natural and progressive, 'ever improving', development, favoured by Darwin.

Mary, the Mother of Jesus, as said, was a surrogate mother, utilised by the 'Angels' to produce their 'emissary' Jesus, an 'Angel' came to her in a blinding light and told her "You will conceive in your womb one who would be great". And nine months later, she duly gives birth.

The drama of Jesus, his birth, his teachings, his rising up into the clouds due to being resuscitated after crucifixion. That he survived, when others died easily on the cross, could not have clearer ET connotations. This is particularly evident with the moving 'craft' accepted as a star, that shone a bright beam of light onto the birthplace of Jesus to guide the three enlightened ones, who must have been made aware previously, that someone of prime importance would be born.

Jesus even survived being lanced by a Roman guard, possibly to hasten his death and relieve the suffering. Jesus was revived by the 'Angels' utilising some advanced process. He warned Mary Magdalene not to touch Him when she caught up with him after He left the tomb. His revival process must have made it dangerous for humans to make close contact.

It may seem strange that ET could have been involved with humanity for such a lengthy period but we have mentioned the proven theory of 'time Dilation', where ET could leave Earth at super light speed and on their return they would analyse, check on the progress, modify or change at will or dispose of the human experimental subjects altogether, if they so wished. However, as said, there must come a time of a culmination, or 'revelations' a time when humans must be made aware of their true origins. As said they missed their chance by not doing this in the Biblical times when humans would have simply accepted it. Surely by now, humans would be well used to the idea.

PILLARS OF FIRE

Amazingly, perhaps they did and in spite of all the aforementioned biblical alterations, the message is there, clearly spelled out in the Old Testament of the Genesis story of Moses and his Garden of Eden. However, we must consider, who told Moses the story? Surely he didn't make it all up; in any case we know he did converse with the 'Angels' but he would have been heavily influenced by the divine classification of the events. The people of those times did not have the advantages that we have, to compare the technology that was displayed in the actions of the 'Angels' to our own capabilities, because in the days of Abraham and Moses they had no technology, therefore beings rising and descending on Pillars of Fire, must be 'Angels' going to and from heaven. So it seems strange that these beings ever allowed Humanity to advance in weaponry over the centuries, with no sign of any reluctance to use them. The 'Angels' of course, would be aware of their own bodily vulnerability. They would have to rely on their advanced protection and defence systems. Which his precisely why they adopt this low profile activity, and not that which was displayed to the Patriarchs in order to control them so easily.

With regard to their aforementioned weakness, it seems strange indeed, that they could cross such vast distances, only to crash on Earth, to have humans capture their craft (and bodies) and 'back engineer' them for great technological advantage, as claimed by UFO enthusiasts. Some indication of this may be apparent in the sudden burst of technology evident in a comparatively short time. A few examples of such may be, heat resistant materials, fibre optics, microchips and nanotechnology, low radar profile and so forth, all arising conveniently as required.

To consider again, their decision regarding when and where to arrive en-masse in their 'second coming'. In the New Testament, certain indications in the scriptures, make it clear that this would occur shortly after the completion of 'Operation Jesus' where he himself stated '"the return is close at hand" before rising up into the clouds. It seems, however, that a major policy decision was made in 'Planet Heaven' to postpone the event.

To complete our analysis of 'The weapons of The Angels', we have to consider how far more advanced they would be in comparison to the use of sonic destruction capability, the Rod of Moses. The Ark of the Covenant and so forth.

If our current UFO phenomena is manifested in beings who may be the descendents of those who decided to 'make' men in their own image, then the startling performance capability of their craft in speeds, manoeuvrability, being able to disappear at will, would make any human resistance impossible.

PILLARS OF FIRE

They have even managed to dodge a laser beam apparently fired from Earth at their craft. An amazing piece of film exists, taken from the space shuttle that shows a flash from an earthly source, then a streak of light fired at a UFO that swiftly turns away into space and the beam streaks through the spot where it would have been, had it not taken evasive action. The fact that we do have a UFO phenomenon, is indisputable, the question is how we interpret it.

CHAPTER VI

ANGELS OF THE ANCIENT EAST

Moses, when listing all the Patriarchs in Genesis and their ages so 'matter-of-factly' mentions this amazing longevity. Noah himself was alleged to have lived for almost nine hundred years, but these excessive life spans seemed to drastically decline in the post-diluvian descendants of Noah. If the theory of 'off Earth entities' involving themselves in biogenetic involvement regarding human origins is true, then they themselves would live for many centuries. Our medical advancements are moving rapidly ahead, along with other technological subjects, so no doubt humans will regain this longevity.

If the antediluvians, that is, the descendants of the early successes, we call Adam and Eve, were destroyed due to faulty behaviour patterns, could it be that this longevity was somehow taken away from Noah's descendants? It would not be acceptable to have future generations living for centuries, if they slipped back into evil tendencies. Who would wish for such people as Attila the Hun, Genghis Khan, Saddam Hussein or Adolf Hitler living for centuries?

The Darwinian conception of human emergence came to a halt with the Neanderthal entities. Their demise may have been purposeful in making way for the obvious improvements in the Aurignacion or so-called Cro-Magnon peoples, who could be regarded as our own true ancestors. There are no links between the true pongid apes and the so-called Hominids and the sparse human bone fossil evidence in no way matches the Darwinian ideal of evolution "Scrutinising, ever improving, rejecting that which is bad and adding up and preserving all that which is good". The bone fossil evidence with regard to humans shows quite the opposite.

Unless some cosmic catastrophe or one of our own making halts human progress we, ourselves will eventually discover a life-bearing planet. This is because we would only concentrate on those in the 'Goldilocks Zone', that is, not too hot, and not too cold and possessing the most important attribute water, which could only exist in a solar system's 'habitability zone'. We would certainly enhance the intelligence of any creatures by advanced genetic means if we possessed this ability, in order perhaps to save them from extinction due to low intellect. The Apes appear to have attributes suitable for advancement in creativity, but only use them for basic survival. Bipedal locomotion still evades them but having hands, manipulative fingers giving them manual dexterity, would, coupled with intelligence and creativity, they could well have been singled out for such a mission profile. Clearly, if, one day, humans will do these things, we cannot disregard the possibility that this occurred regarding our own origins and were given an advanced brain that could envisage, pre-plan, create, invent radio, radar, tabulate the chemical elements, and invent nuclear power. Such attributes are ludicrous to be seen as requests from Simian kind. These attributes eventually brought about the advancing intelligence of our Cro-Magnon ancestors. Initially, they must have been aware of their creators moving about on Earth coming down from the sky and so-forth and this would be the root cause of all Earthly legends regarding 'gods' who came from the sky, preserved by all earthly civilisations passed down to their descendants. At some point, such creations i.e. us should be seen to be fit and ready to be made aware of their origins. This of course was assigned, initially to Moses and his revelations, coached in Biblical terms in Genesis, that obviously were made known to him, that humans were specifically created and enhanced in a special creativity zone called Eden, located somewhere in Mesopotamia, near the rivers Euphrates and the Tigris. Since the waters flowing from The Garden were said to have four heads, a possible location, as said, could be down near the border of Kuwait, between Iraq and Iran, shown in 'The Bible Alive' by Harper Collins. But these four joints are only connections between the main rivers Tigris and Euphrates [p31].

In this 'Garden', they were taught all the positive things, as well as learning all the negative influences. They would be tested for obedience, curiosity and enquiring intelligence. And of course natural reproduction. Eventually, when deemed fit and ready they would have to leave " To go forth and multiply" "Subdue and replenish the Earth".

Unfortunately, modern humans have not entirely followed these instructions, except for the 'subduing' by plundering its resources, polluting its atmosphere and oceans, denuding its forests, covering masses of grass areas with concrete etc. However, all is not lost, humans are slowly waking up to all this desecrating. Greenpeace, Save the Earth campaigners, biodegradable containers and bags, the elimination of plastic and massive recycling programmes.

But for all this, we have to once again consider the 'End Game', that is, to decide when modern day humans, just as Moses informed the Ancients, should be told the true story of their origins, but they would be aware of the enormity of the task, as modern day humans would certainly not accept it in a docile and calm way that the Ancients did. We would not sense anything Holy or Divine in such revelations.

PILLARS OF FIRE

These alleged occupants of the UFOs and their ever-increasing numbers, observations by humans and so many abductees relating their experiences, must see humans as either very slow and dim-witted or being in denial, regarding their presence, when it is possibly phase one of the 'Revelations' operation. Strangely, even the Bible tells of 'Signs in the Skies' when The Second Coming is nigh. It is a long time since 'Operation Jesus' when the decision was made to postpone the Second Coming. 'Operation Jesus' was an excellent plan at the time and one which could easily be repeated on a larger scale. The Creators must have been greatly impressed by the results at the time. An adoring group of followers, even going to their deaths singing, when meeting their demise in a horrifying way to please Pagan Romans. And with a later Emperor and his Pagan subjects eventually converted to Christianity themselves by accepting such teachings (i.e. Constantine).

However, when the promises and forecasts of 'The Second Coming' did not come to pass, the people felt betrayed, resentful and abandoned. They began to see the Apostles and their teachings, even Jesus himself, as false prophets. The wicked and the oppressors would still prevail among them and not be separated out and destroyed, as promised in 'The Second Coming' which they believed would come to pass in their generation.

How did this situation come about? Well, the people, that is, the followers of the teachings were convinced that the day of the 'Lord' promised after the wonderment of the Resurrection and re-appearance of Jesus, would come about after his rising up into the clouds. They were convinced (and told) that their Messiah and His host of 'Angels' would soon return to fulfil the promise. Jesus himself said unto the people "Verily I say unto you, this generation shall not pass till all these things be fulfilled" [Mathew X34]. He also stated "Ye shall not have gone over the cities of Israel 'till the Son of Man become" (returns). The Son of Man of course being Jesus and 'Man' being 'of humanity'. [Mathew X23].

At that time. Israel was a comparatively small country and few large cities existed. But for all that, Jesus was careful not to be specific on the actual date of the occurrence, after such a request by his followers. "No, not the Angels in heaven, but My Father alone", "No man Knoweth of the Time".

St Paul himself was well aware of the 'cosmic' connection regarding Jesus and 'The Angels' having witnessed The Ascension. He made it very clear in a letter to the Thessalonians, less than a generation since the departure of Jesus.

This was AD50 "We who are alive and remain, shall be caught up together with them in the clouds, to meet The Lords in the air" [Thessalonians 1V 17]. Paul also added, "For you yourselves, know perfectly, that The Day of The

'Lord' cometh as a thief in the night, sudden destruction cometh upon them (the evil doers) and they shall not escape".

Although Jesus himself taught the masses to be aware of false 'prophets', He was now regarded as such, by some of his followers embittered by the unfulfilled promise of a 'Second Coming'.

In those times if a prophecy was not fulfilled it was viewed as a serious matter and naturally further prophets and their teachings would be somewhat discredited.

In Deuteronomy XVIII it says "When a Prophet speaketh in the name of the Lord, if the thing that he has prophesied, follows not, or does not come to pass, that is the thing of which The Lord has not spoken".

All this has a very serious effect with many turning away from the teachings. The cosmic connection arises again with the following. "What? Did not this seductor faithfully promise, that he would return victorious in a Chariot of Fire in the clouds? Would we not, at the same time, be changed into citizens of the Kingdom that is not of this world? What has become of these promises and who has seen in the sky the sign of the Son of Man Let us fear The Preachers whose words are not fulfilled as that is proof that they are liars.

These angry words showed the resentment at the unfulfilled promises at the time, but even more so as more than a generation after the departure of Jesus, Jerusalem fell, without any help or assistance from those 'Not of this world [AD 70].

During the prophesies of Jesus, he had also said in Jerusalem to his followers "Seest Thou those great buildings? There shall be left not one stone upon another that shall not be thrown down". This was a prophecy that did come true of course, when the Romans destroyed Jerusalem.

The primary Apostles, Peter, James, John and Andrew kept pressing Jesus to tell them of the signs they will experience regarding the help and Divine retribution regarding the hated occupiers and oppressors of the Jews. Jesus then reminded them of the ancient teachings, in particular the early destruction during the days of Noah. He also spoke of Lot and the Holocaust that befell the citizens of those cities of The Plain. And that a similar fate will befall the wicked when The Son of Man is revealed.

Jesus gave a frightening account of the tribulations to come on Earth and ended with "And then shall appear the sign of The Son of Man coming <u>into the</u> clouds with power and great glory".

PILLARS OF FIRE

He described how The Angels would gather together The Elect (The Chosen Ones). But for all this, the prophecies did not take place when expected. So clearly, a major policy decision had been made in 'Planet Heaven' to delay or postpone this major event. On returning to 'Planet Heaven' after His horrifying ordeal, all his positive teachings as a 'Messiah' during His pre-crucifixion days (that did have marked success) He must have been embarrassed and not a little angry after all the hard work that had been assigned to Him, only to be regarded by some, as a false Prophet. One could imagine Him confronting The Heavenly 'Senate' or decision-makers and making His feeling clear.

However, we must now return to the ferocious activity regarding The Angels of The Ancient East, when they were very active, we would mention again, this great contradiction that Biblical Scholars writers and Rabbis, interpreting the Ancient texts, avoid or never seem to mention or attempt to offer an explanation. The 'Angels' always referred to as the 'Angels of The Lord' obviously operate under the command or control of the 'Lord', since it was the Lord who issued the stern and pious Commandments, including what could be seen as the most important one "Thou shalt not kill" lasered into stone by 'The Finger of God'. How could one of His Angels tell The Israelites during their many battles, when all this killing and slaughtering of The Israelites' enemies was occurring. "Let not a creature that breathes to live?" It is, as we suggested, a way of relieving their own consciences, of a the guilt and blaming it on the directives of the Angels.

When the Israelites finally reached their Promised Land, the battles and killings did not stop. Over the following centuries, their war with the Philistines up to the time of King David and his son after him, (Solomon) The Angels were always there.

However, during 'Operation Jesus' centuries later, no Angels were apparent to save Jesus from His fate and He had not freed them from the yoke of tyrannical occupation. Jesus had only preached love and peace and wasn't seen as a threat or an insurgent by the Romans. Pontius Pilate tried to save Him but the Priests fearful of their future, were happy to encourage the mob to shout 'crucify him'. This took the pressure off the Romans, always fearful of an uprising. It was the Jews that crucified their own Messiah. As for the 'Angels' they were very conspicuous by their total absence.

Any intelligent beings, just as humans, who communicate, would obviously have a name or reference, or perhaps just a number in order to identify such beings to each other in their communications regarding their activities, but apart from the well known Angel Gabriel or Michael, the others, for the most part, were reticent or saw no good reason to give out such information to humans in all those biblical appearances. In fact, one 'took off' literally rather rapidly, after informing one inquisitive human in 'Judges' that his name was not within the 'need of know' of a certain biblical character called 'Manoah'.

In 'Judges' Manoah asked an 'Angel' if it had a name and the 'Angel' replied "Why askest thou thus, after my name seeing it is secret". It was then that the 'Angel' made a hasty departure witnessed by Manoah and 'Judges' continues… "When the flame went up towards heaven from the latter, the 'Angel' of the Lord 'ascended' in the flame of the altar". At this point Manoah and his wife (who most probably had dug Manoah in the ribs and prompted his inquisitiveness by saying "Ask him what his name is") both fell on their faces to the ground.

Clearly they were both very impressed by this 'take off' or 'ascending' to fall on their faces, and here we have a living flesh and blood being (we assume) communicating audibly with humans and obviously human-like itself, rising up on a flame from the 'altar' or platform, to what? It could only be a flying craft?.... as he rose upon his one-man jet pack, that we do know have now been constructed and utilised by humans. Would a divine angel employ such a takeoff method? All our pictures mostly of 'Angels' with 'wings' were most probably the only way the ancients could get the message over, so to speak, that 'they' could rise up into the air, and to depict them with the accoutrements that the birds employ to move about in the air.

The aforementioned 'angel' had not appeared to Manoah just to demonstrate his flying capabilities after a casual chat. It had 'come down' specifically on another genetic implant mission, as Manoah's wife had been chosen to be the surrogate mother of another special biblical character to be called Samson.

Clearly, the creative capabilities of the 'Angels' with regard to their special entities, were improving all the time. The 'Giants in the Earth' in those days' had now most likely been either slain by the Hebrews in the desert, with the help of the 'Angels', or destroyed by the 'Angels' themselves, as now they could create much more human-like entities in stature, but having the immense strength of giants. The 'Angels' already knew the purpose and mission of their creation 'Samson' and that was to deliver the Israelites from the Philistines.

Strangely, instead of selecting an obviously fertile woman, many cases in the Bible occur (Abraham's wife Sarah, for example) where the 'Angels' seem to purposely select barren women (and Manoah's wife was barren) for their creations to be born from. 'Judges', makes it clear that it was Manoah's wife who was itching to know the name of the 'Angel' on the implant mission, which was quite natural seeing it was her that had experienced the trauma of the appearance and implanting operation. Manoah's wife had confided in her husband that a 'special being' had come to her and described its countenance as being like an 'Angel', but the being had not answered her when she had asked of its name.

And so, it came to pass that Samson was born, and it soon became apparent that he had great power and strength by slaying a lion with his bare hands when he reached maturity. Of course, this act pales into insignificance when compared to some of his later exploits, such as slaying a thousand men with the jawbone of an ass and, of course, his well known act that brought the house down (literally) on his Philistine audience. Surely, a very special entity, but nevertheless seemingly bred to be expendable and to fulfil a specific purpose.

If the angels were divine in origin, with all their obvious assistance and interest in the existence of the Jews and must have also been God's creation themselves, it begs the question, was Adolph Hitler, whose mission seemed to be the destruction of the Jews, created by the Devil? Can we have an ultimate divine entity without his ultimate evil and opposite counterpart? It would be rather like having positive with no negative, black and no white, or plus and no minus, and it would seem that we can only believe in both of them, or neither of them.

However, it certainly seems apparent throughout the Bible that the creator(s) could produce entities 'to order', so to speak, to utilise for the fulfilment of their plans, and in this regard they must have been indirectly responsible for the writings of a sizeable portion of the history of the Christian world, but they have ensured it was all written by men and the praise, responsibility or blame, as the case may be, would be seen to fall on human heads, and they would simply remain remote, elusive and mysterious and regarded with awe as ever, and this was, no doubt, purposely engendered and certainly remains true today, if we relate this description to the entities allegedly abducting people all over the world in our own time.

During their struggles and their many battles with the Philistines, the Israelites still had their 'trump card', the Ark of the Covenant, and this deadly instrument had more than demonstrated its powers. However, on occasions it seemed to 'switch itself off', so to speak, as cases occur of people dropping dead for just touching it, and it seemed necessary for it to be carried a full 1000 meters before crossing the river Jordan (Jericho) from the marching columns and then, surprisingly, it allows itself to be 'captured', which naturally would entail close approach and handling by the enemy, totally unfamiliar with it.

When the Ark was left at a place called Shiloh, its power had seemingly 'run down', or had been switched off, perhaps by the 'Angels', because when the Israelites once again called upon it in a battle with the Philistines (related in the book of Samuel) the Ark was captured.

Although the Philistines managed to successfully, manhandle it without detriment, when they took it to the house of a person called Dagon it proved quite fatal to its new host, because Dagon was found the following morning on the floor, minus his head and both hands.

One could easily conjure up an image of Dagon being unable to resist an inquisitive look into the Ark by removing the lid and putting his hands on the edge of the box and peering into it by moving his head over the top, then falling back dead, without his head and hands.

This alarming incident, one would have thought, would have made the Philistines very anxious to get rid of it, but it seems that although they did not know how to handle the mysterious power of the Ark, they still tried to hang on to it and seemed able to move it about from place to place. The Ark seemed to have a will of its own by all this switching on and off with regard to its fatal power, and the Philistines stubbornly held on to it for seven months.

Finally, the Ark was returned to a place called Beth Shemesh, but because someone had looked into the Ark, fifty thousand men died, (even though they were of the Israelite camp) for this dangerous act of folly.

With the return of their secret weapon, which was still secret as no one had lived to tell the tale of what they had seen inside it, the Israelites were finally able to subdue the Philistines under the leadership of Samuel, and the Ark remained for twenty years at a place called Kiriath-Jearim. However, the struggle between the Israelites and the Philistines was far from over.

While the creator(s) and their work force of 'Angels' were occupied sorting out the affairs of mankind in the biblical Middle East sector, and their overawed witnesses were busily writing and recording all the events that seem so questionable to us today, what was going on in other parts of the world where other early human historians were also creating the legends that astound us today with regard to what they were seeing, particularly giving rise to reports of flying shields, flying carpets and 'Vimanas', their power sources and descriptive events of them soaring up into the sky.

The way the ancient Eastern legends are written certainly makes them seem like invented dramatic fables, but it is what may have inspired them, and what may have been observed that is the interesting question, particularly as their recorded observations match rather closely fairly recent reports on the UFO phenomena today.

Is it possible that various popes or high ranking ecclesiastical dignitaries have altered the writings in the Old Testament, or obliterated certain phrases as demonic or un-Christian? If only a few hundred years ago the religious factions were burning people as heretics for scientific postulations that challenged the dogmas, then earlier, the position may have been just as precarious for others less vociferous in their comments.

According to the author Robert Charroux, practically all the popes down to the emergence of the printing presses (which put a stop to it) altered, or modified the Gospels. Many of the ancients, though obviously scientifically unenlightened were well educated and intelligent people, and Moses would most certainly be in this category. Although, as said earlier, the 'Angels' did not care to have their names or titles known to humans, many cases of two-way dialogue occurred in the Old Testament with regard to the questioning curiosity of humans. Is it possible that they did mention that the 'Kingdom is not of the Earth', as the later emissary Jesus had done so? Perhaps they made simple statements of fact to the Patriarchs in answer to possible questions that would be perfectly understandable to us today, but incomprehensible, but nevertheless possibly recorded by the Patriarchs, but later obliterated by the churchmen.

Could we imagine an early pope, or 'Holy See', scrutinising the writings of Genesis and came across something like, "And we travelled between the stars in excess of the speed of light to reach your world from our own planet which has two suns' in the sky". Our evolution began over five million of your years. Almost certainly, anything of such a nature would be obliterated from the text.

It seems quite certain that if the Romans, centuries later, could reduce with no qualms at all, the library of Carthage to ashes, destroying 500,000 volumes and another 200,000 later at Pergamus and Julius Caesar happily disposed of 700,000 valued scientific works in the Alexandrian Athenaeum, a few minor alterations or omissions in the Bible to preserve their divine nature would, at the very least, have been considered.

Later the Caliph Omar kept the fires burning for six months in his destructive rampage through ancient writings, stating simply, "If they are in our sacred book, we know of them already. If they are not, then they are evil and foreign to us". The same ignorance prevailed in humanity right up to the 20th century in burning books seen as a threat to a particular regime.

King David of the Israelites was a wise and enlightened leader and, according to the Old Testament, had discourse with the 'Angels'. He was not averse to calling upon them to assist him in his battles with the Philistines, probably not quite realising that the 'Angels' were, in fact, utilising his services.

In one of King David's communication sessions, he asks of the creator(s) "Will I go up to the Philistines or will you deliver them to me?" The creator(s) agreed to help and said ...."And let it be, when thou hearest the sound of a going, in the tops of the Mulberry trees, that then thou shalt bestir thyself....." This could be interpreted as, "You will hear the trees shaking when our craft is passing over them, so follow up behind". Needless to say, King David won his battle.

And so, it came to pass that, once more the fearsome weapon the 'Ark' was on the move. The chosen ones, who obviously knew exactly how to handle it properly, placed it on a cart for transport to the war zone. However, the driver of the cart, obviously untrained in its potential danger, fearing for its safety as it shook about on the cart, was killed instantly when he put his hand on it to steady it.

The event is recorded in the book of Samuel.... "And when they came to Nachon's threshing floor 'Uzzah' put forth his hand to the Ark and took hold of it, for the oxen shook it, and there he died by the 'Ark'.

King David witnesses this event himself and was naturally quite alarmed and, fearing for his own safety, cries up to the creator(s), "How shall the Ark of the Lord come to me?"....

King David remained suspicious and wary of the Ark and would not bring it into his city, and it was placed in the house of Obed-Edom, the Gittite for three months. King David must have had some reassurance from the creator(s) that he and his city would be safe, as the Ark was eventually allowed in and was placed in the safety chamber of the Tabernacle. To repeat the amazing reference in 'Samuel', where the creator(s) mention their plan to utilise genetic material from David to produce other entities, *after* he is dead. Nathan, the prophet, was a chosen entity and could communicate with the creator(s), and they instructed him to brief King David on their plan. 'Samuel' says ... "And when thy days be fulfilled and thou shalt sleep with thy fathers (death), *I will set up thy seed after thee,* which shall proceed out of ***thy*** bowels".... There is no other way to interpret this other than a removed sperm sample, frozen, stored, then utilised at a later date.

It is clear that there were still one or two genetic freaks around from the creator(s)' earlier experiments in producing 'giants' to fulfil specific tasks, and any offspring from the giants were strangely affected. Perhaps the creator(s)' original intention was to build a super race of mighty beings, but the plan was abandoned after a few experiments after it became clear that they could not achieve their aims in *intellectual* capacity in their larger entities, who always turned out to be brutish.

Samuel says "There was a battle in 'Gath', where there was a man of 'great stature' that had on each hand six fingers on each foot six toes *and he was also born to the giant*".

It seems King David also witnessed a close encounter of the third kind (the book of Samuel is not without its cases of aerial phenomena)..... "Then the Earth shook and trembled and the foundations of heaven moved... he bowed to the heavens also, and *came down* and darkness was under his feet...and he *rode upon a cherub and did fly* and he was seen upon the wings of the wind". Clearly, David was witnessing *some* form of controlled aerial (and quite audible) activity.

It is not surprising that the creator(s) wished to freeze the seed of David to produce further improved entities for wisdom and intellect if his son was Solomon, as history well regards Solomon as the epitome of wisdom and confirms him as a special entity, and when King David died his son Solomon took the crown.

In the Book of Kings, Solomon builds a large impressive house to secure the Ark. No doubt his father, David, had instructed him well in its power and capabilities and clearly, Solomon had great respect for it. The building was some ninety feet long and built to very precise instructions, and took seven years to build. A special enclosure within the main building housed the Ark. No doubt the special instructions included a roof opening to allow the 'Angels' to descend in their 'clouds' because it was not long before they took up residence.

The Book of Kings says..."And it came to pass, that when the priests were come out of the holy place, that the 'cloud' filled the house of The Lord". Obviously the priests had been expecting a 'descent' and all had to leave before it occurred.

When Moses received his explicit original instructions on the building of the Ark, it was stated that the carrying staves should not be removed. However, when it was placed on Solomon's special enclosure, the staves were removed. 'Kings' says, "And they drew out the staves that the ends of the staves were seen out in the holy place, before the oracle, and they were not seen without: and there they are unto this day. There was nothing in the Ark save the two tablets of stone which Moses put there at Horeb"...

Obviously, Solomon was wise enough to have studied the history of the Ark and noted this importance in not removing the staves. Those that had seen the destructive capabilities of the Ark, including Solomon's father David, would have been terrified of disobeying the instructions given to Moses in this regard.

Solomon, however, seemed to interpret this removal of the staves as the secret of disarming the weapon. That he was successful in this, and seemingly correct in his judgement, is obvious by the revelation in 'Kings' of what they found inside the Ark, and the obvious fact that they had come close enough to it to remove the lid and look inside with no detriment to themselves.

An oracle is described in Greek legends as a place to communicate with the 'Gods' and an 'oracle' existed by the Ark in the special chamber built by Solomon, and Solomon did utilise it to communicate with the creator(s).

Solomon, in a ceremony after the installation of the ark, communicated with the creator(s) in Kings… "But will god(s) indeed dwell on the Earth? Behold, the heaven of heavens, cannot contain thee: how much less in this house that I have built?"

This is a most interesting statement and implies that Solomon knew the 'Gods' were from outer space, and he was looking for confirmation that the 'Gods' would live on the Earth (considering all they had done in the past for the Hebrews). He was saying, "Considering outer space cannot even contain you, how can this enclosure I have built contain you?"

Solomon's wisdom is undisputed and with the usual fast travel of the news and interesting events going on in those days by word of mouth across the camel trading routes, the Queen of Sheba hears of the Wisdom of Solomon. The Queen was not easily given to believing any old bit of gossip and took it upon herself to come and see for herself if the stories she had heard were true.

Solomon must have suitably impressed the Queen as she says later in Kings… "How could I have not believed it? Thy wisdom and prosperity exceedeth the fame which I heard". In Kings someone had noticed the possible mischievous spirit in the Queen when she arrived, hoping to expose the exaggerated accounts of what she had heard, and says… "And his ascent (Solomon) by which he went up into the house of The Lord (after she had witnessed it) there was no more spirit in her".

The Queen of Sheba was suitably overawed and impressed by what she had witnessed, which most certainly reads as though Solomon himself could rise up to the observation craft in its 'cloud' equally as well as the 'Angels' could.

The Book of Kings also related to the activities of another very special entity called Elijah, who also was able to communicate with the creator(s) and had special powers. He was able to demonstrate these powers by calling down fire from 'above', rather like a communications infantryman calling up an air strike. He could also demonstrate his power in times of drought by callings down rain whenever the occasion demanded.

PILLARS OF FIRE

A certain action of Elijah in Kings, sees him going to a mountain top (nearer my 'Gods' to thee) to communicate with the creator(s). Kings has Elijah stating… "Behold, there ariseth a little 'cloud' out of the sea, like a man's hand"… This description seems to be his observation of an aerial craft, always described as 'clouds', seen quite far off, to be stated as being small as a man's hand and it was obviously drawing up a huge quantity of water to drop upon the land, which would no doubt be suitably desalinated by some method before delivery on to the land. Shortly afterwards the sky turned dark and, sure enough, down came the rain to solve the drought problem. This event of the craft arising from the sea could equally be interpreted as a craft arising from an undersea base and carrying out some advanced chemical cloud seeding operation that, in some cases on Earth, is utilised today. Some modern day unexplained sightings involve huge symmetrical craft moving underwater and many UFO reports have UFOs coming from or going into the sea.

Elijah was well looked after by the 'Angels', who fed him and provided him with water in the desert. Kings has Elijah communicating with the creator(s) and calling them up for a special task, and they reply to him… "Go forth and stand upon the Mount. And behold the Lord 'passed by' and a great and strong wind rent the mountains".

The creator(s) were obviously quite pleased with the actions of Elijah on Earth as they told him (for a reward?) that he would be taken to 'heaven' in a 'whirlwind'. They must have searched for descriptions of their craft that would enable 'earthlings' to relate to them. However, they made it clear to Elijah, precisely when his transport would arrive and Elijah was able to inform his successor, Elisha, of the fact and discuss it with him beforehand. Those who try to explain away all these events as misinterpreted natural phenomena, would have trouble with *this* event, Elijah *knew* he was going.

Elijah's special powers were well demonstrated as he also had the power to 'part the waters' and did, in fact, do so when crossing over the river to his point of departure. Kings says "And Elijah took his mantle and wrapped it together and smote the waters (the River Jordan) and they were divided hither and thither, so that they (Elijah and Elisha) went over on dry ground". He purposely went across with Elisha to put some distance between them and a watching crowd because he knew that the craft to transport him was coming and, after asking Elisha if there was anything he could do for him before he went, what follows in Kings, is one of the most descriptive accounts of an aerial craft descending to Earth witnessed by Elisha and forever logged in biblical history, "And it came to pass as they still went on and talked that behold there appeared a chariot of fire…" Elisha was brushed aside and Elijah 'went up' by a 'whirl wind' unto heaven.

PILLARS OF FIRE

Now, Elisha had been bestowed with special powers which were clearly related to the 'mantle' of Elijah's that had been left to him, because on the way back he was also able to part the waters of the Jordan. Elisha was accredited with working miracles where his knowledge of mouth to mouth resuscitation, for example, was seen as bringing a child back from the 'dead'.

Kings says "And when Elisha was come into the house, behold the child was dead and laid upon his bed, (a possible 'cataleptic condition) and he went up to (Elisha) and lay upon the child and put his mouth upon his mouth... Eventually, "The flesh of the child waxed warm". Naturally, all those present fell at his feet. Among his other talents Elisha could also cure leprosy. The Old Testament characters and Kings, though witnessing astounding events which temporarily pulled them up short and made them look up again to the creator(s) sometimes, soon slipped back again into their old ways, until the next 'happening' brought them 'back on course', so to speak, and it becomes clear that the creator(s) had a real problem in the process of directing human behaviour patterns that would 'hold', and human kind insisted on slipping back to their more basic and savage instincts. Perhaps the lengthy and ongoing series of alleged abductions still going on today (if all the convincing cases are actual occurrences) are a continual analysis of genetic material (that is said to be removed in each case), in a search for signs of positive genes eliminating the negative, or more savage genes, of the creature originally chosen for the creative events in 'Eden', so long beforehand.

The vision of Ezekiel, is the most well known and frequently quoted event in the Old Testament, that from whatever angle we look at it, seems to be a man struggling to come to terms with a 'close encounter of the third kind', and will not be quoted here in its entirety, but various points in the event can be highlighted.

The ancients had to relate to something they were familiar with when wrestling with the problem of describing the strange and seemingly common manifestations frequently occurring in those times. Whirlwinds were familiar to them and sure enough Ezekiel witnesses 'a whirlwind coming out of the North'. Many UFO sightings, incidentally, seem to either emanate from, or be seen to be departing to, the North and this together with certain early US naval balloon expeditions by a certain Admiral Byrd and later satellite photographs seemingly showing a hole or depression at the Pole, have given rise to theories that the aerial phenomena in our skies originates from, or has a base 'within the Earth itself'.

Where Ezekiel described the beings feet as resembling calves feet, this could be a good description of some form of protective footwear that the 'Angels' would possess when landing on Earth, and would be strange in appearance to a man accustomed to wearing, and seeing others wearing *sandals* most of the time.

When Ezekiel struggled to explain what he had seen with reference to 'wheels within wheels', 'eyes' all around them, whirrings and wings, and so forth, he also stated that the beings of the craft *communicated* with him. Ezekiel was so traumatised by his close encounter, it took him a week to snap out of it and the event is related to 'Ezekiel' in the Bible... "Then I came to them 'of captivity' (slaves?) at Tel Abib, that dwelt by the river of Chebar and is at where they sat, and (I) remained there, astonished among them for seven days".

Ezekiel called the entities that he had observed 'cherubim's' and the word is frequently used in the Old Testament in relation to special beings utilised in the activities of the 'Angels', and so forth. Today our description of cherubim's is probably quite distorted by time, just as our depiction of angels on Christmas cards is also a distortion. The word Cherubim's in biblical times almost certainly had no relation to rosy bottomed babes with tiny wings.

In 'Ezekiel' he says... "And the cherubim's lifted up their wings and *mounted up from the Earth* in my sight"... A helicopter on the ground before starting its engine has its rotor blades in the 'droop' position, then they rise *up* on engine start. The Book of Daniel relates to another special entity (possibly chosen), said to have possessed great wisdom and understanding and once again 'Angels' are on the scene and seemingly protected him in the well known story of the lion's den. In 'Daniel' it says 'My God has sent his angel and hath shut the lions' mouths". Daniel had been discovered communicating with the creator(s) and the elders had reminded King Darius that anyone found affording reverence to anyone else except the King, would, in accordance with a decree signed by the Persian King himself, be dealt with severely, which is by Daniel wound up in the den among the lions.

'Jonah' was another chosen entity of the creator(s), but some of those singled out, such as Jonah, were sometimes reluctant to co-operate and Jonah made an attempt to escape to Tarshish by boat from Joppa, but the creator(s) made the sea very turbulent. Jonah had told the mariners he was fleeing from the creator(s) and finally, being blamed for the rough sea, appears to be thrown overboard to save them. The 'whale' (related here as an undersea craft) that had been following the ship, takes Jonah aboard for three days. Jonah had been 'taught a lesson', and after communicating with the creator(s), Jonah was put ashore and had his original instructions again repeated to him, to 'go forth and try and influence human behaviour patterns in Nineveh'.

At this time, Jonah and the other prophets were instructed to warn people of a special chosen emissary that was the creator(s) final solution for 'the human question', and this would be the emissary Jesus.

Was a great policy change and, indeed a change in the hierarchy, on 'Planet Heaven' taking place? Instead of the pestilences, plagues and smiting of erring human creations, a totally new approach was dawning and the policy would have been transmitted to the creator(s) (by the cosmic voyage controllers) to planet Earth, "Create a special hybrid entity from a chosen human female with special powers to impress by certain actions, gather a following and spread to all lands by teaching behavioural codes and practices to the human creations worldwide, and programme him for the completion of his mission in thirty years". Joseph had not yet married Mary and had not 'known' her, yet she was with child. An 'Angel' plants a telepathic message into Joseph's mind that the real reason his wife to be, Mary was with child before their marriage, is due to their operations. The 'Angel' tells Joseph it will be male and to call him Jesus.

Obviously, Mary had already experienced her visitation by the 'Angels' and the implant had been carried out. Their craft, or moving star, as it was perceived by 'wise men', had been spotted in the East and the word reached Herod, who like the creator(s) had done in Egypt centuries before, proceeded to eliminate the first born male children.

The only moving stars witnessed by earthlings today are satellites holding a steady course in orbit until out of sight, or meteorites with a brief trial. Any moving star that travels about stops, starts, 'shines down' and so forth, cannot be anything other than a controlled aerial craft.

Just as Moses had to attend the obligatory forty day course up in 'a cloud' on the mountain, so Jesus, the created emissary, had also his forty day course, largely on survival and character building techniques in the wilderness, where he was liberally teased, tested and provoked in attempts to get him to use his special power prematurely. Eventually the 'Angels' come to administer to him and it was about this time that Jesus was seen to be fit to commence his mission.

Jesus had shown his special inherited powers when quite young and was wise beyond his years, and seemingly the elders spent more time being taught by Jesus than they teaching him. Jesus goes forth and recruits his helpers from the working classes and began his teaching programme and 'miracles'. It was at this time that the profound policy change on 'planet Heaven' became apparent. Instead of smiting and annihilating the enemies of the Lord, they would be taught to be humble, meek and mild and turn the other cheek.

PILLARS OF FIRE

When Jesus said, "What I can do so ye also can do", was this a clear message that the extra terrestrial genes had been planted in the human brain waiting to be utilised? It is known that humans use but a small part of this fantastic over-endowed organ that set us up as an anomaly, a misfit, a specially created entity light years away in our intellect than any other earthly creation. Are the geniuses of the world a 'thing to come' in all humanity when we begin to utilise all of the brain matter? Although earthly wise ones and teachers preceded Jesus, no one had spoken with such obvious wisdom and intellect by using phrases and examples that his audience could relate to.

During his teachings Jesus implied that the earlier Patriarchs did still exist on 'Planet Heaven', when he said many shall sit down with Abraham, Isaac and Jacob in the Kingdom of Heaven.

In the Bible, depicted in the Book of Matthew, what did the blind men seeking a cure know when they said "Thou, son of David have mercy on us?" It was mentioned that genetic material from David the King, would be used after him to 'produce' a special entity. The Book of Matthew says... "The Kingdom (planet) Heaven is like unto a net that was cast into the sea and gathered of every kind which, when it was full they drew ashore, sat down and gathered the good and cast the bad away". Was this a description of actions on Planet Heaven to weed out the genetically imperfect and eliminate them? The same process *was* applied to Earth's populations at the time of Noah and the flood and.... Sodom and Gomorra, for example. The Book of Matthew goes on to say that the same thing will happen on Earth in their 'second coming', or when the 'Angels' shall come forth. Once again, in the Book of Matthew, a woman makes a clear reference to Jesus as 'Thou, son of David'. Although Jesus was keen to keep out of the political arena, his amazing actions were bound to be related throughout the Roman occupied lands. While the Romans only cared about the political stability of their areas of occupation and not their hierarchy safe in Rome, their puppet governors feared for *their* power and did not care to hear Jesus referred to as 'King of the Jews'.

Jesus admitted that a lot of his cures were nothing more than faith healing, although raising somebody from the dead (depending on how long they had been dead), would obviously be quite different. Someone of Jesus' enormous intellect would recognise a coma, or 'cataleptic trance', which today people have been afflicted by and then 'come back to life' in a cold mortuary after being certified dead, as the life support signs visibly diminish.

Jesus' disciples failed to complete an exorcism, which Jesus did straight away, and when the disciples asked of him "Why could not we do it?", they were told (in the Book of Matthew), "Because of your unbelief", and made the famous 'faith can move mountains' expression. Although Jesus knew he had been 'produced' for a specific purpose and he would be rewarded by being revived and eventually taken to 'Planet Heaven' by the moving craft above, the human side of him manifested itself in the Garden of Gethsemane by wavering before his arrest, "Father, if it be possible let this cup pass from me".

Another manifestation of this profound policy change on Planet Heaven was Jesus rebuking Peter for cutting off the ear of one of the priests' servants arresting him, with… "For all they that take to the sword shall perish by the sword". The creator(s) or God, The Father, had encouraged from above and sent 'Angels' to lead the Israelites into savage massacres of every living thing, including children, in their exploits in the desert, killing happily with the sword.

The last chapter of 'Matthew' makes it quite clear that another 'Angel' descended from the sky, stunned the guards and rolled back the stone from Jesus' burial place. This is related in Matthew… "And behold there was a great earthquake for the 'Angel' of the Lord descended from Heaven and rolled back the stone from the entrance and sat upon it". (This was a 'glowing' entity). The 'Angels' had already removed and carried out the revival process on Jesus. This 'Angel' had only removed the boulder to show Mary (and Mary Magdalene) that Jesus had 'risen'.

After a certain dialogue to his disciples, Jesus finally departs (in Acts of the Apostles) to the same craft that was present at this birth? "And when he had spoken these things, while they beheld he was 'taken up', and a 'cloud' received him out of their sight".

A prophesy of the return of the emissary Jesus, in the *same manner as he went,* was clearly stated by two entities in white suits, or apparel. "Ye men of Galilee why stand ye gazing up into heaven? This same Jesus which is taken up from you shall come so, in like manner as ye have seen him go"… The creator(s) (as part of the operation where the ones that Jesus had recruited must go into all the foreign lands to preach) had to infuse and telepathically insert the ability in them to speak all foreign tongues, and they did this at the first opportunity that they could, when all the Apostles were together, and the beginning of 'Acts' Chapter Two says, "And when the day of Pentecost was fully come they were all with one accord in one place. Suddenly, there came a great sound from 'Heaven' as of a rushing mighty wind and it filled all the house where they were sitting". The result was that they could all speak in foreign languages which, no doubt, would be very useful to them when they began their travels.

What was the beam of light that fell on Saul on the road to Damascus, and the voice from 'Heaven' that rapidly converted him? It can clearly be seen that the Bible is replete with celestial events and close encounters, which were (and this would be encouraged by the instigators) taken as divine events. 'Heaven' to them was above in the sky, and anything happening above them that they could observe or hear audibly, such as 'voices', 'thunderings' and lights flashing forth, pillars of cloud, pillars of fire, were all heavenly inspired and therefore divine in nature.

Clearly, with these beliefs abounding on Earth, it was comparatively easy for entities descending from above to find willing humans to do their bidding while in awe of 'Angels' from Heaven. In our 'enlightened' times the only thing 'up there' is space and quite obviously, if these 'Angels' are now still around, then they would know of our awareness and would keep well clear of us. We must ask what period of time have 'they' decided upon, or have 'they' decided upon a conclusion to it all? When will humanity be seen as fit and ready to receive 'their' revelations? Will it be, as Nostradamus predicted, when a great 'King' will come from the skies?

CHAPTER VII

PILLARS OF FIRE

The Old Testament is almost entirely taken up with the preoccupation of the Hebrew peoples with their own importance in the scheme of things, and all the events, wanderings, battles and struggles are all centred around this aforesaid preoccupation with their promised land and their struggle to occupy it.

However, if such a fantastic event, as the purposeful genetic creation of earthly life forms, did occur by extra terrestrial entities, they would have, as said, been quite active in other areas of the world as well as the assumed area of initial creation (that is, the Middle East). If the aforesaid creation event produced our immediate ancestors, which may just be the Cro-Magnon peoples, then it is little wonder that the anthropologists are so perplexed at the lack of evidence to link Cro-Magnon with his supposed predecessor, Neanderthalensis Sapiens. Furthermore, we can now put some kind of date on the alternative creation event as happening somewhere between thirty five and 100 thousand years ago, and generations of the alien creators would have been present afterwards engendering the flowering of humanity, up to the time we started to actually record our history.

Certainly, a lot of 'subduing' and 'replenishing' and 'tilling the Earth with the sweat of their brow' would have had to have taken place before the inherited advanced brain of the developing human could begin to reflect on more higher pursuits. One only has to see the garden, once proudly trimmed, of an empty house after a few months of neglect to imagine what the profuse vegetation and foliage of the Earth would have looked like to entities arriving on a 'Planet of the Apes' one hundred thousand years ago (the onset of cultural evolution is stated as forty thousand years ago but anthropology has been attempting to push back the appearance of Cro-Magnon as far as possible, on meagre bone fossil evidence).

The huge monsters, most of which were herbivores that had stripped all the foliage so avidly so many millions of years before the Pongid apes appeared, had all long since disappeared and, although other foliage eating animals existed on Earth, the apes could be choosey, they picked only the fruit and berries and nuts and did nothing to 'subdue and replenish the Earth'.

During the dinosaur era we may wonder how the growth of the foliage could have kept up with all the hungry mouths. Now the situation would have reversed, the foliage was swamping the animals and the apes would simply climb above it and did nothing to deplete it. Our so-called ancestors had only been equipped by evolution with enough instinct and grey matter to simply ensure their survival and nothing more and had no creative ability whatsoever. However, their body form with certain modifications, seemed fairly suitably *equipped* for creativity *it if could be utilised* for the emergence of a more refined intelligent creative entity.

Clearly then, the creator(s) (as the Bible confirms) *would* see their first priority as instructing their creations to 'subdue and replenish the Earth', and would ensure the wide dispersal of their created entities to go forth and multiply on all the lands of Earth.

Human evolutionary concepts tend to view Africa as the birth place of humanity, but that is where they may have trekked to, rather than originating from. It has been suggested that the Babylonians inherited their knowledge from the Hindus spreading from the East and possessing advanced knowledge long before the Babylonians.

Where did ancient Tibetan wisdom come from or the Chinese and Japanese cultures.

Did the mythical 'Lemuria', the alleged birthplace of **all** the Asian races, once exist? Whatever the earthly race, they mostly seem to have one common denominator in their own legends, and that is their 'creation' long ago by 'gods' or sky people and, of course, the Christian Western World's people are no exception. Our legend is the account in Genesis.

Did the legends all stem from the mixture of racial memory and also the interesting observations of aerial activity as the early transported human creations paused to wipe the sweat from their brow during all that tilling, subduing and replenishment of the Earth that the creator(s) had instructed them to do?

The legends would be added to and embellished and distorted over the generations until finishing up similar to those in the Mahabharata. Of course, earlier, they would have to be content with depicting the 'gods' of the sky with a solar disc with wings attached to it, but as time rolled by the mining of metals began (perhaps telepathically induced) their legends would begin to mention 'flying shields' and so forth, as they tried to relate the phenomena to things they were familiar with.

There must have been an enormous, but gradual build up of knowledge over the centuries preceding that which apexed some four thousand years ago in Egypt, but where did it occur? Was it the antediluvian cultures (preceding the flood), giving the Egyptian culture the impression of having somehow 'sprung' into existence in an interesting comparison to the appearance of the Cro-Magnon entity, who was the real human ancestor rather than the poorly endowed and uncreative ape, or the brutish Neanderthal.

Certain circumstantial evidence seems to indicate that a lost land mass may have been the original creation zone of the early human, and not Africa. Although having been a favoured area of early humanity, they may have concentrated there after arriving on its western coast from a land mass now lost but once existing exactly where the ancient Egyptian priests said it was, in the Atlantic Ocean.

Whereas modern charts divide the Pacific Ocean with our 180° Longitudinal Line, the Egyptians seemed to have divided almost exactly the land masses of the Earth for their possible zero Meridian and, whereas ours passes through Greenwich in London, theirs seems to have passed straight through a pyramid and the Nile, some 30° East. If so, this implies a knowledge of the Earth's global land masses and the existence of atlas type charts, and a knowledge of the spherical nature of the Earth. Such charts were probably consigned to the flames long ago together with all the other knowledge, making our past a closed book.

It is said that Columbus was a collector of ancient charts and quite probably was well aware of the spherical nature of the Earth. He seemed quite certain he would not sail over the edge of the Earth, as some of his crew obviously feared. However, the wise Columbus realised that it would (in spite of the perils of the sea) be safer to **prove** it rather than risk being burned as a heretic for any risky pronouncements.

It seems quite amazing that it should even be considered that the Earth was flat some two thousand years after the ancient Greeks mathematically proved the spherical nature of the Earth.

Really, it is not surprising that the ancient Greeks knew the Earth was a sphere, as they would have acquired much of their knowledge from Egyptian sources and their great repositories.

I said in another work that the hidden knowledge suggested in Coptic texts as being secreted away in the pyramids by the priests, may only be a few blocks down from the pinnacle. If we consider the smooth limestone cladding that was added, then with the gradual removal of the ramparts, it would be utterly impossible to assail that area and tomb robbers, with gold and treasure in mind, broke their way in at the bases of the pyramids. Of course, now that the limestone cladding has been largely stripped off, a new attempt, perhaps utilising some form of X-raying programme (seemingly confounded in the past utilising natural cosmic particles) may provide interesting results.

It is stated that the pyramids radiate energy. There is an interesting account rendered in a work dealing with the activities of lost, or so-called Ante Diluvian, or pre-flooded peoples by Rene Noorbergen regarding the Pyramid of Giza. It seems that just before the turn of the century, the British inventor, Alexander Siemens, climbed to the very top of the pyramid with an Arab guide. The guide noticed that when he stretched out his arms he experienced a ringing in his ears. When Siemens followed suit he felt a tingling sensation. Guessing it to be an electromagnetic force, he moistened a newspaper he had with him with the contents of a bottle in his pack, wrapped the newspaper around the bottle, then he had a so-called 'Leyden jar' to accumulate electrical energy. He held it above his head and shortly sparks began to fly out of it. The Arab guide thought it was witchcraft and tried to pull Siemens' arm down. At that point the force was directed toward the guide and knocked him off his feet, whereupon he bolted and was never seen again. The pyramids have produced volumes of suppositions and conjecture, but still retain their mystery.

It would appear then, that by the time the 'Angels' were motivating Abraham less than four thousand years ago, they had already seriously established themselves on Earth and in the affairs of men.

As said, our ancient past seems closed off to us. Not only is there this reticence to get involved in what some works call 'Ooparts', or out of place artefacts, but when we do try (and the pyramids are a good example), we seem unable to comprehend their actual significance. There is certainly a vast amount of circumstantial evidence for ancient technology having existed, and the inspiration for it all may be directly traced back to the influence of our *hypothetical alien creator(s)*.

As said early in the work, the flood event may have been utilised rather than caused by the creator(s) wishing to save selected correctly functioning entities, who seemed to 'measure up' to their desired standards, so as to continue with their procreation programme after things settled down again, but then we would have to ask what caused the flood? A massive comet? A huge asteroid into an ocean, or even the *arrival of the Moon*? One thing we *can* be sure of is that marine deposits and shells exist in the highest mountain regions of Earth, but the question is not quite answered whether they are direct evidence of a worldwide flood or deposited when they were seabeds long, long ago, and the secret would be in accurate means of dating them.

If we measure the onset of the more sophisticated civilisations commencing with the mining out, smelting and working of metals, we are still in trouble, as when we think we have a good approximate time for this achievement, along comes another 'Oopart' to confound us. The well known machined cube found in a coal seam is well documented to the less well known intricately tooled and worked silver 'vase' blasted out of solid fifteen feet deep rock during quarrying operations in Dorchester, Massachusetts in the 1850s, *and pre-dated the accepted appearance of humans on the Earth.*

If we see a fossilised creature in rock, such as a fish with every bone in place, the significance of this does not immediately occur to us. However, when the fish dies, it sinks to the bottom of its habitat and, if not immediately eaten, quickly decomposes and the bones all disintegrate and drift apart to finally (given sufficient time) form chalk deposits, such as the White Cliffs of Dover, with all that calcium. For a fossil to be so preserved it would have to be immediately covered by massive alluvial deposits forcing out all the oxygen and compacting with the weight of continuing deposited material to form sandstone, then rock and eventually preserved for all time as a fossil.

Which leads us to believe that other traumatic flood events had occurred long before the biblical or Babylonian accounts were assumed to have occurred? How did the Egyptian priests come by this information that they related to the visiting Greek travellers, such as Herodotus and Solon where they stated that catastrophes, such as Atlantis, had occurred many times on Earth, and even spoke as though they were aware of the 'precession of the Equinoxes' by stating the Sun did not always rise in the position it did then? The twenty six thousand year wobble as the pole rotates around the zodiac, has the Earth now entering Aquarius but some suggest that the Sphinx was built in the age of Leo.

If the flood legends can be said to be fairly likely to be based on archaeological facts, perhaps our other legends such as those relating to human creation by 'sky gods' also have their roots in fact. It is said that not one civilised race of people exists that do not trace their origins back to 'god(s)' or the 'creator(s)'. To go to the root of it we may ask why did they bother in the first place? The answer may be that having advanced to the point of being 'gods' themselves, then their purpose was solely to create and, hopefully produce in their turn, more creators, simply to continue the process and this, in our case, has happened.

The fantastic intellect given to human kind from whatever source, divine or extra terrestrial will, if we survive, ensure that human kind will become cosmic creators. There is nothing more certain. To be sure, if we had lived through the enormous evolutionary period of the fifty million years existence the apes have had (who have never created anything), we would already be cosmic creators. Fifty million years of existence, and they still swing in the trees or jump about in our zoos, yet it is still seriously suggested that the human brain is a bequest from them.

The aforesaid paragraph, in my opinion, reduces the options on human origins to divine or extra terrestrial forces being responsible for human origins. The process of natural evolution is not disputed per-se, but only with regard to the human entity on Earth, evolving in natural line from apes in a traceable bone fossil display, which of course is nonexistent.

As said, if we do survive our own actions, or any 'celestial' threat (for which we have absolutely no protection in spite of our technology, enabling us to annihilate ourselves), we will, without doubt, be carrying out the actions it is postulated could have happened here on Earth, and that these actions could have happened on Earth is reinforced by the mass of data that is already firmly logged in earthly legends, myths and writings which, of course, clearly include the Bible.

The explorers of old looked with amusement at natives worshipping the Sun. It did not seem to occur to them that this is a more natural act than worshiping any other objects, artefact or mythical being from our various legends. The Sun is life. It sustains all life on Earth. What could be more logical than for the primitives to worship it. Our very bodies are made of star material. To suggest other intelligent life does not exist in the cosmos is now seemingly preposterous and, as soon a man set foot on the Moon of our young world, the possibility that other intelligence in the cosmos could not be capable of space flight seemed equally preposterous.

With regard to earthly legends seemingly referring to 'sky gods' and celestial events and 'initiators' from the skies, it seems all laid down as though factual and unquestionable, however, our aims and developing ability to travel in space ourselves, postulations in this regard must emerge on the simple basis of the aforesaid, "We can, so they must be able to", since many off earth intelligences are bound to be more advanced than ourselves in our comparatively 'young' solar system.

Early man should have only been preoccupied by his own survival – hunting, fishing, planting, gathering and protecting his family. He should not have even been aware that the twinkling stars were other suns, let alone thinking about 'sky gods' and creators.

A mere few hundred years ago supposedly learned men were saying such things as, "Don't be ridiculous, there are no 'stones' in the sky therefore stones cannot fall from the sky", or "The world was created in 4004 BC", or "That it is flat", and all the ancient Egyptians, Greek and Chinese sages with their logic, studies and teachings seemed to count for nothing, and it is only in comparatively recent times that our technology has moved forward in such a rapid burst of advancement in such a very short time period.

What put the concept of 'star men' and 'sky gods' in the heads of the ancients if they were not based on actual happenings? It does not seem to be something that would be concocted for no apparent reason. We can now concede to the possibility of 'star men' arriving in earth space because of our knowledge of the cosmos and that the possibility does exist. Surely, as far as the ancients were concerned, the stars were no more than small points of light in the sky.

What planted the racial memory of 'gods' being responsible for creation? They would have watched childbirth and noted the similarity to their animals' birth process. Theoretically, they had no reason to suppose that they were anything more than a cleverer species of animal themselves. Nevertheless, the 'star men' are there, well established in all those legends. Long before the 'aliens of Abraham', celestial beings were seemingly well entrenched in earthly affairs.

If mankind were actually created by off-Earth Intelligence and Cro-Magnon men were the result, it would certainly answer a lot of questions, and it would solve the anthropologists' problems because they still have not found the links to establish the Hominids to the true Pongid apes, or down toward Homo Habilis, the so called toolmaker, or Homo Erectus, alleged to have human type qualities, or Neanderthalensis Sapiens.

The question is, if we are a genetic experiment or creation, which subject did they choose to breed us from? There are genetic similarities in simian kind compared to humans, but then, could we suggest pigs are genetically similar to humans? Their material is used in heart operations. We could also look at the dissimilarities in apes to humans, the pelt, the jaw, the teeth, the skull, the long arms and short legs, the different hands (thumb arrangement), the hip joints that prevent them being fully bipedal, their feet, their lack of voice equipment and, finally, their tiny and very unhuman brain, with no creativity, no imagination, no intellect and no desire to be anything but an ape, and any suggestions that they could have bequeathed the fantastic human intellect to Homo Sapiens is preposterous. To speak of chimps having 95% if similar genetic material as humans, common earth worms have 60% similar genetic material some types even posses 80%.

Could the hypothetical alien 'creators' have chosen Neanderthal as their subject? They lived in family groups and supposedly buried their dead. It is not certain that they had fully developed speech, but they would have communication of some sort as do gorillas and other primates.

However, in spite of our positive gifts, we have a dark side and cannot seem to stop going to war with each other. Our whole philosophy seems to revolve around conflict and struggle. We 'fight' disease, we 'conquer' space, we battle against the elements, we struggle to survive, and war seems to have existed as long as humans have existed, so where does our aggression stem from? We do not see armies of gorillas or apes forming up on a field of battle, so is it fair to blame them for our strange savage traits? If Cro-Magnon had not appeared on Earth, the apes would have re-inherited the planet, as Neanderthal, if anything, seemed to be 'retrogressing' rather than advancing and seemed like an evolutionary dead end. Our own creation legends in the Western world relate to our 'maker(s)' stated, "Let us 'make' men in our likeness", so we must assume that the aliens did resemble us and were quite easily able to masquerade as 'angels' and move freely among humanity in those times, but we have the 'greys' to consider, we are not created in their image, are they simply interplanetary allies of the humanoid 'angels'?

I have said in another work that the list of elements should be finite and that there are bound to be life forms far different to us in the way they are made up, but surely they will be the same basic start stuff in their atomic structure as ourselves? Our geneticists must surely agree when reviewing their own fantastic speculations, what a race of beings, perhaps thousands of years ahead of us, would be capable of. Perhaps the reason for the aggression in humans, is a reaction 'they' have not yet fully controlled when extra terrestrial genetic material met with simian type, and that this could be a reason that such material always seems to be removed from the many alleged victims of the abductions, simply for analysis for any advancement over the millennia. However, to return to the humanoids and 'greys' working together, American Forces in Japan worked together as two of the racial types making up humanity, i.e. Caucasian and Asian (the third being negroid). If 'they' created humanity, then 'they' and their descendants would be responsible for it.

They certainly seemed to feel quite responsible for us in biblical times when slaughtering all those misfits and destroying their iniquitous cities in those far off times.

How can the devoutly religious accept a divine creator who is perfect and infallible when the universe contains such horrors as comets, meteors, asteroids slamming into the planets, ice ages, colliding galaxies, exploding stars, and so forth. Intelligent life forms 'out there' must be going through indescribable horrors and some of them may have departed their own world and may now be on their way towards ours.

PILLARS OF FIRE

With regard to our obvious warlike and savage behaviour, and given that it is not such a preposterous suggestion that alien entities may exist in earth space, can we conclude what the alleged abductions are really all about? This factor of the constant monitoring of human tissue must surely be a significant factor. Was the introduction of extra terrestrial genetic material into the human gene pool the cause of this chemical reaction in producing the unique human Jekyll and Hyde syndrome, where we can soar to great heights of intellect and scientific achievement on the one hand, and plumb the depths of depravity in the other, with neither gaining dominance except in cases of lunacy or genius?

The 'culling of defective or degenerative entities in the Bible seemed necessary to the 'angels' then, because the negative genes had gained dominance and they were 'begatting' like-minded individuals. Later, with those selected to be saved 'they' appeared to have restored the balance. However, in the case of Lot and his family who were from Sodom and Gomorra themselves, although it was only in the 'gate', Lot's wife totally disobeyed the 'angels' commands and paid with her life. Then lots' daughters, who for some reason wished to 'preserve his seed' go to bed with Lot and both had incestuous offspring, so if they were among the selected 'righteous' beings, it may give us some idea what the other citizens were like. Perhaps lot and his family would have perished if they had not been related to Abraham.

The worrying point is, what are the current policies of the ruling body on Planet heaven today? Have they just finished their party conference there? Did the 'human question' come up? How do they view their creations today, with the drugs, crime, children kidnapped, raped and killed, old people mugged for a few pounds and left battered, the mutual hate over religion in Ireland and the Middle East and the former ethnic cleansing occurring in Bosnia and Africa where people lack the simple ability to co-exist with each other, the oppressive totalitarian regime in the East and formerly in the USSR, the organised crime bosses, murderers and constant wars of humans somewhere on the globe? Things may not bode well for us if the regime on 'Planet Heaven' regain power as they had in biblical times.

Put the case that, after all this time of their involved existence, even the resources of their long ago terraformed planetary neighbours are now also diminishing, when watching us pillaging and damaging the Earth, might they just decide to take it for themselves? Perhaps, as suggested previously, their metabolism reacts well to additional ultra violet rays and the depletion of our ozone layer is a purposeful act by these watchful creators to condition the world for themselves.

They may have become quite fond of Earth and view it as their 'home from home', and long for the halcyon days of their early creativity programmes and distributing us around the world to subdue and replenish it with the sweat of our brows, and unknowingly instilling the initial racial memories of 'sky gods' creating men in some great garden.

There is some evidence to assume that Moses did 'plagiarise' older Sumerian texts when writing the Old Testament, but the events nevertheless, still seemed to have happened with 'extra terrestrial' connotations still intact. In the epic of Gilgamesh the following will be quite familiar to excerpts from Moses' version. "No mortal comes to the mountain where the gods dwell. He who looks the gods in the face must die". Although Moses had many audiences with the creator(s) he never actually managed to ride around in their craft, unlike his predecessors such as Enkidu from the epic Gilgamesh, which on one tablet read like an account of a trip in an aerial craft with the 'eagle' asking him how the Earth looked from on high. Enkidu's reply was a pretty good description of how the ground looks from a good height, with the sea looking like a lake and ground looking like' porridge'.

A few scientists studying the ageing process are considering the possibility that the extreme ages, stated so matter of fact in their manner in the Old Testament, may have some basis in fact with regard to the makeup and metabolism of the antediluvian, or pre-flood, peoples. I asked earlier in the work if the creator(s) could produce people that lived for upward of nine hundred years, how long do they themselves live?

To refer again to the epic of Gilgamesh, which has more extra terrestrial connotations than the Bible, Gilgamesh is seeking the realm of the 'gods', "Gilgamesh, wither art thou hurrying? Thou shalt not find the life that thou seekest. When the gods created man they allotted him to death, but life they retained in their own keeping".

I said in the introduction that in spite of our wondrous technology and promise of things to come, the present is positively dull in relation to what was seemingly going on in the past, and this is particularly relevant in regard to the Mahabharata and the Ramayana. Rama travelling in 'celestial cars', aerial battles, missiles, etc., all 'tall tales' (we assume) but what inspired the 'celestial cars' and Indra's golden flying chariot? "Silver swans by Ramas bidding, soft descended from the air, and on Earth the chariot lighted – car of flowers divinely fair". 'Flying carpets', 'flying shields', 'chariots of fire', in unfolding 'clouds' of thunder – the past is steeped in 'flying sorcery'.

I have said before that even in 100% fictitious novel is based on life's actual experiences and occurrences, so where did the ancients get their inspiration from when describing all those flying craft?

With all the advancement our possible creator(s) have achieved since those far off days, it is not so surprising that their craft are now so silent, or can dematerialise, and make inertia and gravity defying manoeuvres and disappear before the very eyes of aircraft sent to intercept these radar detected 'blips' that come streaming into our airspace and stop dead over specific areas, only to disappear derisively before the very eyes of the frustrated interceptors. 'They' have even displayed a sense of humour and wound up on the tale of intercepting jets, and nothing the pilot did could shake them, who usually they gave up trying and headed for home.

Although the Middle Eastern Patriarchs chose their own land and the longest river they could find for the approximate location of the human creation centre, if we put ourselves in the position of the creator(s) arriving on the 'Planet of the Apes', as the Earth was if we choose the period of 100,000 BC, would we choose such massive, wide open hostile continental area? If we wanted initially to 'coral' our created entities for behavioural checks and tests we would have to pen them up like cattle for fear of them wandering away. Perhaps the tenuous link with Atlantis and its theorised loss beneath the sea is the basis behind the racial memory of the flood and, instead of the waters coming up; it was the land going 'down'.

The meaning of the word...... Adam is said to mean 'red', or made from red clay. The American Indians, whose legends refer to this island of creation where all the tribes once existed, also speak of the red man being 'made' in the ovens of the 'gods' and turning out 'just right', and not like the black men, which were overdone, and the white men who were 'underdone'. If the island was situated where the Egyptian priests told Solon it was, then initial created entities would be transported across to the nearest adjacent continental land mass, i.e. Africa, the assumed birth place of humanity, and South America.

To refer again to the Sumerian epic of Gilgamesh, he tried to reach the abode of Utnapishtim, who was described as the 'father of men', but the 'father' lived on the far side of a great sea and no craft flew across it except those of the 'gods', but he does finally make it across this sea. Furthermore, he is warned of a great flood to come and he was given the task of building a boat just as in the Noah story. However, it would appear that his boat was not the precisely constructed vessel more akin to an ocean going liner that was so precisely conveyed to Noah by the creator(s).

Many things would have to be considered by one man in constructing a vessel that should have involved teams of experts in maritime design skills, and although the instruction regarding the 'dimensions' of the vessel seem precise in the writings of Moses, the detail involved in other considerations would have required a third book of Moses, or a Genesis III. The food supplies for not only the animals that would not spoil or 'go off' would have been an enormous problem on their own.

Not only would they have to be sufficient to last the voyage before the abatement of the waters, they would have to last to feed the animals and human occupants to the point of arriving on dry land severely contaminated by seawater that would have needed enormous cultivation, *to start producing again.*

In order to take on board two of every species of animal, the three decks mentioned in Genesis would certainly have been required, but how was access afforded between decks? One could hardly imagine the animals going up and down the stairs that are built into our modern ships. Perhaps Noah designed lifts with sacks of fodder for balance weights, with ropes and pulleys.

The problem in that regard would not be insurmountable, but what of *the most profound problem,* that of ship's lighting? The whole design, planning and mammoth effort in constructing the Ark and saving humanity and Earth's species would have gone for nothing had there been a fire at sea, and so firebrand lighting would have been an enormous risk and surely not considered, but what alternative had the ancients at their disposal? This is an interesting question and certain references in old accounts and legends quoted in other works seem to indicate that the ancients had knowledge of a form of chemical lighting that they employed quite extensively. Why are there no carbon deposits on the walls of the pyramidal tunnels? Not only for the prolonged building process where they could hardly be expected to hold firebrands in one hand and work with the other, but in their detailed ceremonies where the same problem arises.

If the ancient Egyptians were clever enough to produce the pyramids themselves, which still baffle twentieth century technology, then the problem of lighting may have been easily overcome. We think that 'electro plated' metals and the process of 'galvanising' were introduced in the early part of the nineteenth century, but what about the much written about ancient batteries unearthed in Baghdad and attributed to the Babylonians? Evidence exists that electro plating was going on around 2000 BC.

Professor Denis Saurat has found evidence of electrical devices used in ancient Egypt. References have been made to some kind of ever-burning lamps utilised by the ancients. Greek and Roman writers have referred to them. Even St. Augustine says, "Neither wind not water could extinguish it", when referring to another ever-burning light in an Egyptian temple dedicated to Isis.

PILLARS OF FIRE

Andrew Tomas says "During the Middle Ages, a third century 'perpetual' lamp was found in England it had burned for 'several centuries'. Also, when the sepulchre of Pallas, Son of Evander (immortalised by Virgil in his 'Aeneid') was opened near Rome in 1401, the tomb was found to be illuminated by a perpetual lantern which had been alight for more than two thousand years".

The scientists of old were termed 'magicians'. They kept their secrets of natural methods (now scientifically known and discovered) to themselves and certain writers, such as Rene Noorbergen, suggested that an enormous amount of discoveries had been made and utilised by the antediluvian races that were entirely lost and destroyed and had to be relearned by future races, and Noah, of course, would be the last, together with his family of the so-called Antediluvians. Is it possible that Noah could have been further assisted by the creator(s on landing, as strongly as their assistance towards his survival at sea, by providing explicit instructions for him to construct his survival vessel?

It would appear that the ancients relied more on their mental processes of memory rather than written details for everything they did. Moses, when writing the Old Testament accounts in Genesis, displayed amazing feats of memory when recording all the descendants' names and ages at death of the biblical characters.

After the alleged global deluge, it was down to Noah to reintroduce practically everything all over again – a formidable task for one man and his family. Could Moses have written so explicitly and precisely about all the characters and their descendants if the whole thing was a fabrication? There would have been absolutely no point in it. The provisions, marketing and facilities to introduce a 'best seller' did not exist in those days, so clearly there was no possibility of financial gain. As said in the introduction, archaeological discoveries have vindicated biblical sources in the past and we cannot disregard it completely as all fabrication or 'interesting' yarns.

It is interesting to note in regard to the biblical destruction of supposed malfunctioning 'creations', that the 'Bambala', an African tribe, relate in *their* legends that a 'former' human race was destroyed by the 'gods' because they had been disobedient and useless.

The concept offered in this work is that strong circumstantial evidence exists (aided and abetted by biblical writings) that humanity *could* have been created by extra terrestrial intelligence, initially to 'subdue and replenish the Earth', as suggested in Genesis, and that all earthly legends appear to retain the main ingredient of this possible occurrence, but modified by their own additions, omissions or embellishments. If such a fantastic event did occur then the creator(s), with all their assumed expertise in genetic manipulation, have been responsible for the mystifying and hugely over-endowed human brain for the excess of brain material still awaiting its turn to flower into being in our skulls.

Their enormous patience and possible perplexity, together with all the alleged abductions, may be a manifestation of their concern that the negative traits in our makeup have not been consumed by the emergence of this additional material still not becoming activated, except for certain signs in some gifted individuals, *and it may be of some concern to them.*

The only answer to the question, why should 'gods' bother to create man in the first place, must be to become creators ourselves and to eventually take over the role and to then descend on pillars of fire on far off worlds and create and direct life forms upon them. So... why was man created? The answer to this question may be adequately contained in Sumerian legend... "So that he might bear the burden of creation".

There is a report in an ancient Babylonian text in Cuneiform style from the time of Hammurabi, the 'created' ones, or servants of the 'gods' rose up against them in rebellion because of their labours, and that the perpetrators were annihilated after they had dared to threaten 'Enlil', Lord of the atmosphere!

It certainly would not appear to be logical that humans, with our own self-esteem and obvious superiority over other life forms, should 'naturally' choose to consider ourselves in all those legends as subservient to a greater lifeform or a hierarchy of 'gods', or that we were created by a God or 'gods'. On the contrary, it would have been more logical to have seen ourselves as gods over the Earth with our obvious dominions over all other earth creatures. Unless, of course, certain things had been *observed* in the sky, for example, that clearly showed the existence of a higher lifeform to 'look up' to and, since so many earthly legends *do* contain references to such 'gods' and their 'creating' of humans, it is logical to deduce a common denominator to it all at some point in our remote past.

Before the introduction of writing we may have utilised more grey matter within the memory cell regions that may have since 'atrophied' and may still be doing so since the introduction of calculators relieving us of the neurological stimulus of mental arithmetic. However, by the time the introduction of writing occurred, all the various creation legends that were previously handed down by word of mouth (and consequently embellished and distorted a little with each telling), finally became settled into book form, such as the Christian creation legend of Genesis. Humans will be the creators of future worlds, starting possibly with Mars or Venus, and our predecessors may have passed this way billions of years ago and introduced the blue/green algae into the Earth in its primordial state that we can find in rocks of the Earth that are *three and a half billion years old*. Soviet scientists, after their tremendous achievement of a soft landing on Venus, have calculated that only a period of around six hundred years would be needed to change Venus into a liveable habitat for our descendants. Although the conditions on Venus today seem fearsome in the extreme, they would be equally extreme on Earth three and a half billion years ago, yet the blue/green algae obviously survived to enable the process to get under way.

Although we are conditioned to biblical and Hebrew writings referring only to a single Almighty creator, the Hebrew word 'Elohim' is a plural word, perhaps this influenced the puzzling phrase, "Let us make men in our image".

The Greeks and Romans may have been much nearer the truth than the later Christian rendering with all their gods up in the clouds and on the mountain tops, and the Greeks, as said earlier, had their 'gods' creating life forms in the underworld. The Genesis account suggests that the creator(s) also produced the life forms of Earth in their creation zone of Eden and had Adam their human creation name them all.

Earthly legends suggests 'sky gods' brought certain crops and cereals to Earth and, in this regard it is interesting to note that certain seeds and grain, if left to their own resources, would simply die out. One example is maize and there is a strange analogy in this factor when we consider how helpless humans are at birth and if humans suddenly adopted the attitude of the animals of the field and left the offspring to fend for themselves, the human race would cease to exist.

How can we explain the similarity of many earthly legends being so similar and well rooted before humans had even built the means of travel over vast expanses? This is only one of many unanswered questions regarding our past.

To return to our own creation legend, that is, the Bible, how can anyone reading the Exodus account, concerning solely the Hebrews' 'promised land' adventures, fail to notice the breathtaking hypocrisy of the dramatic events leading up to the emergence of Moses from the mountain top carrying his tablets containing the Commandment written in stone, "Thou shalt not kill", when the creator(s) 'passed over' the Hebrews' houses and annihilated every new born Egyptian child and, what's more, sallied forth ahead of the Hebrew army in many battles and sanctioned the outright slaughter of every man, woman and child, and in some cases everything that lived in those defeated cities.

PILLARS OF FIRE

These hypothetical creators would surely not be acting under their own volition with regard to their actions and policies on Planet Earth. They must have, on their own world, some form of hierarchy, or ruling body that formulates their policy and actions on faraway worlds. One assumes the wholesale slaughter was sanctioned by that far off world, or even in 'Heaven'.

Also, in Heaven we are taught that there is a hierarchy of angels with ordinary angels that we could assume are all aspiring eventually to become 'arch angels'. Is this the way to the top in Planet Heaven? To be utterly ruthless with regard to any life forms that they themselves are said to have created on far off worlds, such as here on Earth in biblical times that may stand in the way of their aims and achievements?

Whereas a cool, advanced intellect, acting with pure logic and completely devoid of passion or emotion might utilise the aggressive genes nurtured in their creations as a means to an end, or in other words, to do their bidding with regard to their aims, plans and earthly operations, it is very hard to believe a divine, faultless creator could sanction such killings and slaughter of the innocents, let alone sending 'angels' to go before them, or even providing lethal weapons like the Ark of the Covenant, or a 'death trumpet' that could break down twenty-one feet thick walls.

The Hebrews, who did so much moaning and complaining during their sojourn in the wilderness, with their frequent exclamations of, "We might as well have stayed in Egypt", surely would, after all the aforesaid drama of the receiving of the Commandments, have notices that they were breaking at least one of them *continually*, that is the aforesaid "Thou shalt not kill", and would surely have made some mention of their possible concern about it to Moses.

Why didn't the creator(s) promise some unoccupied land instead of an occupied land to the Hebrews? Why not in the middle of the Sinai? After all, the city of Nevada nestles in the desert quite happily with its underground water source and, since all the creator(s) had to do to produce water for the masses was to instruct Moses or Aaron to strike a rock to produce water, then the water problem could have been easily solved.

Why was it necessary to slaughter all those people in seemingly needless battles over all those years to attain a coastal strip of land at the lower end of the Mediterranean?

The original tablets with the Ten Commandments on them were thrown down in disgust by Moses when he observed the Hebrews worshipping the golden bull. Although the creator(s) supplied him with a fresh set later, what happened to the *old* ones? They would have been trampled underfoot and ignored and covered with wind-borne sand. Would an archaeological dig, or a concentrated effort, reveal them at the base of Sinai? At least we have an *approximate* area to start looking. It seems then; they had their last known resting place in the Ark residing in Solomon's temple. However, as said the Ark's actual final resting place is open to question.

Although the past seems hazy or inaccessible to us, we can produce remarkably accurate clairvoyants to predict the future, but not to unravel or solve the mysteries of the past. Tiahuanaco still goes totally unexplained. Volumes have been written about the pyramids, but we cannot state that we fully understand their meaning.

The aforesaid bell-shaped object composed mostly of silver, intricate leaf work on it blasted out of the rock seam, was dated as *several millions of years old*. Then there is a pre-Inca object made from *platinum,* a material that requires 1755° Celsius to melt it. A Chinese metal belt fastener comprised of 85% *aluminium* from AD 265–316 found in the burial site of a Chin Dynasty general in China, when aluminium was supposedly not successfully produced until the early 1800s.

A high quality machined steel cube with a precisely cut groove around it and other items, such as a gold chain found in coal from the Carboniferous period, iron poles in India that do not corrode, evidence of atomic blasts in the remote past, ancient forms of lighting which were not firebrands. Electric batteries and electro plated artefacts, patterned boot prints found in stone. Atomic theory discussed in 500 BC, Babylonian priests knowing of Saturn and Jupiter's moons in 2000 BC, markings designed to be seen *only* from the air. So much has been written about them they have become boring, yet *all still go totally unexplained.*

Given enough time after a worldwide cosmic or nuclear holocaust, with the earthly processes of decay, corrosion and erosion, all our modern day technology could disappear, only to emerge here and there as a series of puzzling events, legends or 'Ooparts', to baffle future archaeologists and scientist, and this seems to have been well confirmed with the record statements of the ancient Greeks when some of their countrymen visited the wise Egyptian priests.

We cannot have good and evil cows or good and evil pigs or birds. We only have good and evil people. We cannot relate savagery in animals to evil. A cheetah will tear another animal to pieces to survive. We devour animal flesh (such as beefsteak) in a much more refined way having scientifically killed it beforehand (also as part of our survival process), but animals do not line up on the battlefield. Apart from occasional aberrations to the positive or negative, we seem to be held in a balance of negative and positive forces in equilibrium. If we *were* divinely created it would have been a simple matter for a being capable of waving an airy hand and stating 'Let there be light', and created *everything* in seven days, to have eliminated all the negative forces and produced a world of perfect beings.

If we assume that, he did not do this as it would have been utterly boring for him and lacking in challenge, we can only assume we were created *for* amusement and challenge. Equally, if advanced extra terrestrial creators *did* create the human entity, giving rise to all those earthly legends, then we could assume that *they* also, with such advanced knowledge, have eliminated our negative and destructive traits. The fact that they did not do so only serves to reinforce their fallibility and imperfection in being unable to precisely control genes and behaviour patterns.

We could assume, as I have previously suggested, that genes, their predictability, mystery and control thereof, could be the greatest problem and challenge to the advanced creators, or that they are in full control of them and *purposely* created us in this form. After all, some aggression and not a little savagery has put certain people, such as Alexander the Great, Julius Caesar and many others in the history books for all time, and these do seem to be the qualities of certain 'go getter', aspiring managerial types, climbing over everything and everybody to reach their goals and aspirations. We, ourselves, may eventually create purposely aggressive entities long into the future for certain specific purposes, such as military operations. It is quite possible that the death rate from boredom would be higher and a world full of saints than on a world such as ours. If we needed these qualities to set us off on the road to achievement and advancement in the past, have we now reached the point when we *no longer* need them, and in fact, they begin to *retard* our advancement? Would the creator(s) then see a need for further 'stimulation' of the positive genes? Would this be part of their programme after their 'second coming'?

Religious teachings say we are given the choice of good and evil and we can either roast or rejoice, the choice is ours. However, if we are only supposed to till the earth with the sweat of our brows, raise our families, put back as much into the earth as we take, live, die and go to Heaven after life on this Earth alone, there would be no need for the savage and aggressive qualities. Equally, there would be no need for curiosity, wonderment, abstract thought and creativity either. In short, we would be living apart from the tilling and planting, much like an ape or gorilla colony.

Clearly, we were created with higher pursuits in mind, but this still does not rule out a divine creator, because when he said 'Go forth and multiply', he did not 'qualify' it by saying 'on this Earth only', and in the future we will almost certainly be going forth and multiplying on earths we have shaped and moulded in the so called terraforming process for just such a purpose.

And where will this all end? A final conflict or challenge to the creator himself? When we have discovered all the elements and particles and can create all life forms and matter we will be as equal to the creator(s). *Now* the two entities begin to merge, the divine and the extra terrestrial becoming almost as one and the same in our imagination making us choose whichever is most comfortable to our thought process. What then? Is there a ceremonial changing over of power. The old tutor expires with 'May the force be with you', and then we travel the universe creating until confronted finally, in our turn, by our own advanced creations far into our future.

It does not seem possible to believe in a divine creator without believing in an ultimate evil, or a devil, or Satan, and an opposite to Heaven that is commonly called Hell. Most modern theologians now seem to reject the 'Middle Ages' concept of a devil or Satan. Even the Catholic Church, once happy to condone the burning or drowning of witches, is now loathe to assign devils to possession cases, preferring to see them (except perhaps in extreme cases) as mental aberrations, and even in the extreme cases the exorcism is condoned on a 'nothing to lose' basis and where psychiatric treatment has failed, perhaps the confused brain will respond to ecclesiastical methods to right itself.

It would be preposterous to expect all assumed extra terrestrial Intelligences to be above aggression, war and savagery, but those among them *that may have achieved interstellar travel,* and highly advanced creative abilities, would surely not have achieved such status if they had not eliminated most of these traits, at least to some degree, perhaps by 'mental evolution', for the want of a better term, with the futility of war and aggression having finally dawned on them.

Although humans still slaughter each other on the battlefield, we do so on a much more infrequent and smaller scale than we did in the days of Alexander the Great or Julius Caesar, by the time we do achieve interstellar travel we may just possibly have weaned ourselves away from the habit and look back on them as part of our advancements to mental maturity. In that mode of thinking, long into the future when <u>we</u> live for hundreds of years, *we* may be 'tolerant', to a degree, when observing the antics of our *own* creations on some far fling battlefield on another world.

If then, the descendants of our assumed creators are still noting our behaviour patterns and examining our genetic advancement in all those abductions, how do they view our *current* mental advancement? Perhaps, when reviewing the actions of their *own* hypothetical forebears when carrying out the orders of the particular regime on Planet Heaven with regard to human elimination, they are more inclined to tolerance of *our present* activities. For example, in Isaiah 37:35, it states, "Then the 'angel' of the Lord went forth and smote in the camp of the Assyrians one hundred and eighty five thousand; and when they (The Hebrews) arose early in the morning, behold they were all dead corpses". The Hebrews apparently slept through it all and had no hand in it whatsoever. The 'angels' took care of it and did all the 'smiting'. Why so quietly? And with what? Some kind of neutron bomb? 184,000 people are roughly equivalent to the casualty list of Hiroshima.

What was the 'Bull' that came 'out of the sky' in the epic Gilgamesh and annihilated eight hundred people before being killed by Gilgamesh and his friend Enkidu?

What was the Greek poet Pindar really saying when he remarked, "Of the same lineage are men and 'gods' and both draw breath through one mother".

With regard to the 'angels' of Exodus, it is an interesting question that if accepting the fantastic assistance rendered to the Hebrews to the attainment of their promised land, where the 'angels' went forth ahead of the Hebrews and 'smote their enemies in their camp', why were they so conspicuously absent or reticent to assist the tragic Jewish people who went to their deaths in their millions in all the Nazi concentration camps?

Conversely, with all that obvious aggression in the Sinai, why did the Jewish captives seem to accept it as their lot to be systematically destroyed, even assisting their captors to heave the corpses into the ovens when they fought to vehemently under Moses and, in fact, do so today to protect their hard won status?

We could ask the question, is it possible today to imagine a group of armed guards to get a crowd size of a division one-football crowd, to strip off and march into the gas chambers? At the very least there would be riotous panic on the basis that they had nothing to lose.

Where were the creator(s) and their angels during the holocaust? On a spot of home leave on Planet Heaven? Or was this part of the 'new order, or new policy directive or no more direct interference in earthly affairs? This would serve the purpose of allowing our history to retain such horrifying events in order that we could possibly be made to look back on human actions in the future. Is it possible that Moses blamed all the mass killing on the 'angels' simply to ease their own consciences? Did the 'angels' utilise the Patriarchs and their Hebrew army to achieve their objectives on Earth, or did Moses blame all their slaughter and atrocities on the 'angels'? It would take a Crown Court to sort that one out.

Moses was not the only infant that suddenly appeared floating in a river tucked up in a basket. King Sargon I, for example, (3000 BC) was also found in a bamboo box in the Euphrates. The natural conclusion is to assume that Moses simply copied this event in his writings with regard to his own birth.

However, we could equally assume that it was a favourite ploy of the 'creator(s)' to adopt such tactics that played heavily on the human qualities of emotion and sympathy. If a slaughter of the innocents was going on how could anyone pull a child from the river and kill it? The natural reaction would be to *save* it and having done so, *continue to protect it*.

The circumstantial evidence seems to suggest that whenever the creators wanted a special being for a specific purpose they simply chose a suitable female (either virginal or barren) and carried out their implants as required.

If the character in the Sumerian legends called Gilgamesh, actually existed, he also was a special kind of being. He was born of a daughter of King Enmerkar of Uruk. The 'gods' communicated with him and informed him that he should put his daughter into a kind of quarantine by locking her up in a tower. Later she bore a son who became the hero Gilgamesh. Clearly , the creator(s) did not wish to risk her having any romantic encounters that may have interfered with their plans to produce their own entity.

There are other similarities in earthly legends that beg the question, were the later versions simply copies and embellishments of earlier accounts? Heracles, an ancient Greek hero, was another special being and just like Jesus was taken 'up' by the creator(s) having completed his earthly mission, and his remarks were strikingly familiar. Before being taken 'up' to Heaven by Zeus, he said, "Father, I come, it is finished". Clearly, a very similar phrase was attributed to Jesus after his earthly ordeal and ultimate rising 'up' to the 'cloud' or craft awaiting him.

The Bible assigns enormous longevity to some of its characters and as the human lifespan is seemingly becoming longer and longer with each century that passes, it would be natural enough to assume that if accepting the existence of extra terrestrial entities, who may be thousands of years in advance of humanity, then they may well be able to bequeath longevity to chosen 'creations', but even in the case of Abraham and Moses who were comparatively short-lived, they may have lived on for enormous periods in the realms of the creator(s), having finished their earthly tasks, perhaps forever, one cannot die twice.

PILLARS OF FIRE

When Jesus took his Apostles Peter, James and John up a high mountain (always the realm of the creator(s)) Jesus transformed into a gleaming white entity, which may have been simply a reflection of a strong light source to prevent the Apostles from observing the craft. A man from biblical times observing the bright neon ceiling fittings we are familiar with would appear to him as magical.

The Apostles, although not observing the craft, clearly observed Jesus speaking to the *still* living Moses and Elias. However, since the Apostles had never met these Patriarchs that lived centuries before them, they would not have been immediately aware of who they were and Jesus would have had to explain this to them later, since there is no mention of the Apostles being 'introduced' to them. Naturally the disciples were quite afraid as the usual large cloud, with the dramatic voices emanating from it also occurred in this account.

These entities in the mountain tops certainly seemed (if they were not divine) to exploit the naïve and unsophisticated ancients who were only too willing to assign such activity to 'gods' or 'angels'.

So much time has passed since the amazing events related to the Bible and since the wonders of construction, such as the pyramids and the South American edifices were built, to try and unravel it all and make some sense of it would be rather like starting a jigsaw puzzle with a third of the pieces missing. If we *had* every scrap of knowledge from all the afore-mentioned destruction of manuscripts and scrolls would, humans now be descending on a mountaintop on a world of Tau Ceti impressing the emerging intelligence that may exist there? Tau Ceti is a very sun-like star and attended planet are now being discovered regularly.

We would be happy enough to be assigned the title of 'gods' if it suited our purposes and made our plans there easier to achieve. The possibility of the ante-Diluvian races, or Earth peoples existing before an earthly holocaust such as a global flood, having reached a high state of technological advancement, is hinted at in certain legends and all those 'Ooparts', and it seems to be borne out by a statement from the lips of Solomon himself when he said… "There is no new thing under the Sun, is there anything whereof it may be said 'see' this is new? It hath been *already* of old time, which was *before* us". Clearly, Solomon had access to texts, scrolls and writings (probably now destroyed) that enabled him to make such a statement.

Scientific advancement and cosmic awareness has almost certainly introduced disturbing thoughts and doubt into once comfortably accepted doctrines. Christians are taught that Christ died for humanity on the cross and so, in order to accept the scientifically computed possibilities of other world

Intelligences which are assumed to exist, did he, or is he still going through that appalling ordeal for all those *other* assumed civilisations?

We could easily discount the idea of other world Intelligences (which in any case do not seem to be talking to us after fifty years of S.E.T.I. or Sky Search programmes), and reflect on the possibility, as some scientists are now considering that it is *our* mission to go forth and multiply as we were initially instructed. A comforting thought for humanity. However, the odds against such a hypothesis are utterly enormous.

A great strain is being imposed on the doctrines of divine creation by cold, logical science and it began with the fear and discomfort induced in the Church elders by Galileo and others, some of whom paid with their lives for introducing doubt and uncertainty into the entrenched Christian dogma.

If the law of averages is borne out, humanity should be due for another profound discovery similar to the Dead Sea scrolls. This possible 'find' may be very profound. The discovery may be the aforesaid Commandments cast into the dust by Moses when encountering the graven image of the Hebrews. It might be the Ark of the Covenant, a petrified cross wrapped in a type of Turin shroud with the story of Jesus indelibly inscribed upon it. It might be the complete skeleton of an ancient human ancestor, half human, half ape, vindicating all the enormous labours of the anthropologists, their much sought after and indisputable 'missing link'. It may equally be the remains of Noah's Ark or an artefact that could be clearly defined '*not of this Earth*'.

The wise sages of old, responsible for all those profound writings that were ultimately destroyed would surely (if they were all that wise) have made a copy of two of their great works. Perhaps they did, as some documents exist in museums that are completely undeciphered. The first scientific chemists (or alchemists) guarded their secrets and knowledge jealously and were called magicians, or MAGI two of which visited the birth of Jesus and most probably did secrete copies of their discoveries away, duly signed to immortalise themselves in the eyes of future generations, and the Russian poet Valery Bryusov summed it up quite well with his verse, "The poets and sages guardians of the secret faith, hid their lighted torches in deserts catacombs and caves".

Although there would be no point in telling a mountain climbing casualty this, the force of gravity is a comparatively weak force. Birds do not defy it, they 'overcome' it with their muscles and wing form. Balloons utilise the science of physics and the properties of hot air or gas which is lighter than air. Aircraft need forward thrust and an aerofoil shape that simply reduces the upper surface pressure in comparison to the lower. However, it we could discover a substance that would 'insulate' us from gravity, rather like a sheet of material between two powerful magnets that defies their attraction, then we could shout 'Eureka!'

Science is working on the problem and possibility, in time, they may discover an effective method of overcoming this universal force. When (or if) they do, then the usual hindsight they will be surprised why they did not realise the answer sooner. If you don't consider gravity is a weak force, the entire mass of the Earth can't pull a magnetic figure off my fridge door.

The power sources seemingly utilised by the 'angels of Abraham' seem a curious mixture of advanced aerial ability, which kept their silent cloud covered craft aloft for all those 'angels' to come down from and rise up to, but they were not above a bit of booming and roaring which implies crude, earthly thrust in their mountain top activities, but perhaps these were simple acoustics to frighten the ancients and make them susceptible to do their bidding. Whatever their power sources were, they obviously had dangerous side effects to humans who were warned often enough to stay clear.

Human scientists may not find a gravity defying material, but a breakthrough in clean nuclear fusion, or perhaps anti-matter propulsion would see the spacecraft designed for interstellar rather than solar missions coming off the drawing board, then it would only be a matter of time before our 'flying shields' were being observed by some other world Intelligence.

The aliens of Abraham, if they ever existed, are now centuries ahead of their abilities of those times, and so we should not be surprised that they can apparently not only defy correct identification in their manifestations to us today, but also defy inertial forces and dissolve their mass using some form of 'anti mass' field generation.

When discussing supposed profound knowledge of the ancients of antediluvian races, Andrew Tomas who wrote about such matters, says, "Some of the most incredible tales of antiquity concern levitation or the power to neutralise gravity. It is that by using their 'Chaldean magic' by means of sound, the priests of ancient Babylon were able to raise into the air heavy stones, which a thousand men could not have lifted".

Today, in some massive construction enterprise, we would not even consider cutting out a stone sixty feet long, fourteen feet wide and the same thickness in depth as we simply could not lift it, but the ancients did, and the evidence is there to see in the Temple of Baalbek in the Lebanon which the Romans conveniently utilised as a foundation. Also (and this involves huge stone constructions elsewhere) they were quarried from afar. Andrew Tomas also relates that certain Arab sources mention curious tales where the pyramidal stones were wrapped in papyrus and struck with a 'rod' by the priests to make them weightless for the final positioning and in this regard if the stones of the pyramids were levered, heaved and juggled into position, one would expect the fine sharp edges to be chipped and marked and show evidence of this, *but they do not.*

Modern day magicians can certainly fool us today and their task would have been much easier in ancient times, and magicians have always been with us, but how do we separate myths and magic from factual events.

A recent television programme dealt with a team of people, whom we may refer to as 'de-bunkers', that travelled through India to convince the superstitious masses that the wise men were misleading and fooling them, and the mission was an attempt to bring the masses into the twenty first century and prevent exploitation of gullible people for monetary gain. However, while attempting to engender disbelief no illuminating explanations were forthcoming in the programme. For example, how the Indian rope trick was accomplished, or the vitrified solidified glassy rock that only a nuclear explosion could have caused, or the tales of ancient Indian warfare actually utilising weapons that sound very nuclear in their fury, all of which remain unexplained today.

It certainly would appear that with regard to explaining what was going on in the past, clever modern day science is at a total loss, but, as said, how can we complete a jigsaw puzzle when most of the pieces are missing?

CONCLUSION

What was it all about? What is our conclusion? Can we assign a simple process of elimination to it all? We could ask, did the biblical Patriarchs actually exist in the first place? If we agree that they did, we would have to ask, were they all liars? This would not seem likely, so we are forced to ask, did they actually have all those close encounters with beings that they were happy to accept as 'divine angels' of the Lord? Were they 'hybrid' creations specifically bred to be subservient to their creators?

If they were not assumed to be liars, or 'tellers of tall tales', the Patriarchs had very close encounters with beings that were not of this Earth and, as said in the introduction, heaven most certainly is not of this Earth, therefore those beings were most certainly 'extra terrestrial'. To consider former biblical alterations, their origins may have been mentioned.

The final question must be, *were* those beings 'divine' in nature? Obviously to adequately answer this questions we have to look at their alleged actions and activities on Earth in the days of the Patriarchs and other biblical characters, and that is precisely what this work was intended to do, and the most inexplicable event is the aforementioned massive reversal of policy from the Old Testament to Jesus in the New.

Our pre-conceived notions of how a divine entity should, or would act, *could not*, be in any way applied to the activities of the 'angels' in the extracts from the Bible that are included in this work. However, what we could conceive from them is a direct involvement in the affairs of humanity, deciding who is fit to live or die, and going about the annihilation process of it in a cold, detached and ruthless manner that the only conclusion can be, 'they' are responsible, perhaps for our *very creation*. Such a project as the genetic creation of intelligent entities from a less endowed lifeform would be an enormous undertaking and inherited responsibility of the original creators' natural descendants, and it is entirely possible that the 'angels of Abraham' *were* those descendants. If they had the ability of super light speed and our suggestions regarding time dilation and so forth, a creation event that took place perhaps many thousands of years ago, would not entail millennia of constant and patient observation but could be carried out on various missions, after enormous periods of elapsed time on Earth that would not necessarily apply to 'them'.

This would allow for a situation existing today where this continuing interest and analysis of human development appears to be *still continuing*. How would they view the results of this ancient but ongoing plan? Well, we are still here at the moment and we are achieving great things, and will very soon enter 'their' domain by leaving our solar system, either as an extended eye of a nuclear powered probe or our own bodyforms.

Has our modern day technology pushed back their 'front line' continually? If they are under the ocean our submersibles and bathyspheres go deeper and deeper. If they are at the poles we mount excursions there. If they had a huge mother ship in orbit, where does it now reside as we have been there also.

Did they construct bases on the Moon giving rise to all those astronauts talking in code regarding their observations there. Were 'they' responsible for all the T.L.P., or trans lunar phenomena of white and coloured lights moving about on the Moon, and huge symmetrical machines seen 'working' the crater rims (Chapter Seven refers) and photographed by N.A.S.A. Now humans have been there too. It has been seriously suggested that the once active Moon programme, with talk of bases and mining expeditions there, was abruptly terminated after Apollo 17 because N.A.S.A. found evidence of *an alien presence there*.

Perhaps they reside in the Brazilian rain forest being worshipped all over again by the natives as 'gods'. They would know that those natives keep well away from the rest of humanity so there is little likelihood of them coming out to tell us. Many convincing reports and photographs originate from that area. Now we are encroaching upon them again by chopping down all the trees there.

With regard to the Northern Pole, many reports of aerial phenomena have craft streaking northward. On the rare occasion when the North Pole is cloud free an enormous depression, or hole, has been photographed. Do they reside *within* the Earth?

If we postulate that such a profound event of extra terrestrials as being the creators of the human race, at least some of the representatives of those beings would *still* be evident in earth space. Were those creatures, said to have been retrieved in the New Mexico Desert, just such representatives? Will there be a second coming? Profound revelations? A great king from the skies? This would certainly be in accordance with the Nostradamus prophecy. If so, we had better listen.   The severe and punitive actions in sending down plagues, pestilences and abject cold-blooded murder of innocent first born and wiping out entire cities, may not be a thing of the past to 'them' even though it is to us.

Human behaviour patterns must perplex them greatly to have instigated such a fantastic policy change evident in the doctrines of their emissary Jesus. Has their hypothetical mission been successful? If they wished to create beings, who would become such, ultimately themselves, then it has, providing 'they' overlook our obvious imperfections (and there are a lot to overlook).

If they wished to eliminate humanity and start all over again they could do it in a much more subtle way than the methods evidently used in biblical times. The depletion of our protective ozone layer (that we blame on ourselves), for example. Or, if they did wish to return to their crude, but effective ways they could simply guide one or two of the larger asteroids toward us. Even though we have the technology to possibly prevent the annihilation of the human race, we have not done so. Yet we would happily put up orbiting missiles to gain earthly superiority if *other nations let us get away with it* – surely a strange thing?

Now our intelligent radiations are sweeping over possible worlds to a distance of around eighty to ninety light years into space. Can we be sure no aggressive entities, that may be worse than humans, do not reside there and may be on the brink of interstellar travel? Could they now be busily deciphering our broadcasts? Even if none of the suggested events in this work have happened a major event may *ultimately* occur, after all, they know 'hotel Earth' is now open! And the lights are on, with the welcome sign illuminated.

Otto Binder, a onetime N.A.S.A. communications expert, wrote a book (together with Max Flindt) called 'Mankind, Child of the Stars' (Coronet), that seriously proposed, in a very convincing manner, that human kind *are* 'hybrid' entities, produced long in the past by 'star men', who decided to create humans in their own image. This was a bold proposition twenty years before the, even bolder (but true) propositions our own geneticists are *now* making, with regard to our own current and future genetic creational abilities.

If we consider the whole question of human origins and firstly disregard the unlikely possibility that life on Earth is simply a biological 'accident', then we are left with *divine creation, evolution from the primates,* or possible *genetic creation by off Earth Intelligence.* Taking the first proposition i.e. divine creation, we could assume an almighty god stated 'Let there be light', and the big bang occurred, but we could not assume he was an infallible being incapable of making mistakes as out in space there are exploding suns, colliding galaxies and, closer to home, comets asteroids and meteors threatening out very existence. Also the Genesis account for divine creation is to incredible for our logical processes to accept in the fashion in which it is written, yet many people retain their beliefs and ignore the puzzling 'seven days' clause that Moses may have misinterpreted.

With regard to our natural involvement from the primates, we have creatures swinging in the trees with a tiny brain and who have never created anything after fifty million years evolution, yet supposedly having bequeathed the fantastic creative brain to human kind. Furthermore, a century of digging and searching has failed to produce the evidence to support it that is unquestionable, and anthropology remains the most contentious and controversial of all the sciences, with every bone fossil claim disputed.

Clearly, the genetic scientists of today, astound even themselves with their discoveries, could not logically refute the capabilities of an 'off Earth' Intelligence, thousands of years ahead of us and possibly arriving on an earthly 'Planet of the Apes', long in the past, yet not being tempted to enhance the intellect of the primates, with having the capability to do so. For all that's been said, 'the third alternative' is seemingly, as things stand, the only logical conclusion for the three main assumptions for human presence on Earth (until a conclusive and totally convincing discovery is made to vindicate a specific theory). However, can we relate the astounding possibility of the third alternative to what appears to be happening in earth space today, that all the victims of the alleged abductions may have (4,000 years ago) called 'angels'? There still seems to be a strong interest in humanity for some profound reason today, with regard to the many close encounters and alleged abductions with U.F.O.s roaming freely in our skies.

If the abductees are all dreaming and the strange aerial phenomena are natural manifestations, not all understood, then where is everybody? Our S.E.T.I. programme have searched the skies for many years with no results (that we have been told about). The last remark, in brackets, is not so strange, when we consider the strenuous activities of the authorities to withhold all that data on UFO reports and obliterate large amounts of the data when they finally had to release them, to be more outgoing with information on extra terrestrial signalling us. This gives rise to the supposition that 'S.E.T.I.' could have been set up as an expensive ruse to be seen as searching, therefore *not having* actual evidence, or little bodies being examined somewhere *very remote* on Earth today.

How many signals wafting over the Earth from deep space did we miss during the immense existence of the dinosaurs, or all the time leading up to S.E.T.I.?

We mentioned the patriarch Moses and his proclamations in Genesis, that some of his pronouncements may have been influenced by other writings, such as the 'Babe' in the Basket episode, being so similar to that of the story of the future king Sargon 1st. He was drawn from the River Euphrates as a babe. However, his statement regarding the scientific fact that the 'waters' was the medium that brought forth the "moving creature that has life" is quite astounding and is mentioned much later in historical writings.

PILLARS OF FIRE

Every era in history has its enlightened scholars, who may have also studied the great repositories but may well have been unable to access such a volume of work, if it was after the pillaging and burning through ignorance. Therefore, much more data would have been available for Moses to have studied (or to have been taught), than later historians.

The Sanskrit Book of Manu, second century BC states, "The germ of life first appeared in water due to the action of heat". This agrees with the scientific viewpoint that the heat was the lightning bolts striking the waters that caused the chemical reactions, necessary for the creation of the amino acids and eventually DNA and cells. It goes on to say, "It manifested itself as a plant (seaweed?), an insect, a fish, a reptile, a mammal and finally in the form of man".

The ancient Greeks also supported the view that life began in the waters. "Man's procreator was a fish. Living creatures came from the waters".

It may at first, seem strange, that writing as appearing from such widely diverging areas, but it gives rise to the suggestion, that simple copying or previous data took place, but we must remember, that it is written, that scholars from all over the known world, travelled to the Alexandrians library, to study but, Moses, as said, would almost certainly have had access to a greater volume of knowledge than later scholars. Today, no one could read every book in the modern library and in the 'Pre-pillaging' days, there were said to be many thousands of works, therein, clearly, the priests and scribes would have tutored Moses in the most pertinent ones. Of course, a very important historical discovery was unearthed in the east, many clay tablets where found and much information was revealed in Cuneiform form fashion rather than scrolls.

The important point is who was the original tutor (or tutors) that inspired people to write all this mass of knowledge. Stories of ancient teachers, who came to earth long ago, or out of the seas in the case of the Persian god 'Oannes', and the South American areas, also had 'tutors' that where worshipped by the Maya and other people of that area. To return to the scientifically accurate proclamation, regarding water and life. Science today, puzzles over the 'ooparts' or out of place artifacts, seemingly from impossibly ancient periods, this clearly indicates, that it was the people of those times who where the artisans of these ancient objects and also the original scribes that enabled the writers of all those scrolls to record it all for posterity. The problem that now arises, is rather like the chicken and the egg, who or what came first?

If the ancient tutors had all this knowledge about the mysteries of life, they must also have had laboratories, advanced instruments, electron microscopes, knowledge of microbes and germs, obtained seawater samples, studied the DNA and cell structure of living things and so forth. The other alternative mentioned is that the tutors where the ancient astronauts, suggested decades ago (and now again in vogue). Their original planet may have all the conditions in place on their world and in times past, it may have gone through all the processes that our world was subject to, in short, they were the original 'creators' of humanity that saw it as their clear duty to teach their newly enlightened subjects all this information, and the ability, to write so they could record it all for future scholars, with the ultimate aim that their creation would eventually become creators themselves. Certainly they would have instructed humans on the mining and excavation of metallic ores, such as iron, copper, bauxite for aluminium and so forth. This of course gave humans the first giant leap as mentioned in the work, to eventually construct spacecraft, and finally the great event of July 1969.

Of course, the alternative argument would arise again, that we tend to underestimate the abilities of the ancients. For example, an open cast area of iron oxide, exposed to the fury of the elements particularly during a storm and several lightning strikes, witnessed by local humans. On inspection, they notice solidified bubbles of iron and after examining it thought how useful it would be for this hard metal to replace their breakable stone artefacts.

The natural process from this, would be, to apply their recently discovered use of fire, for smelting and eventually the manufacture of metal objects and then weapons, the defend from and hunt down animals and of course to partake in the defence from and to attack, other human groups, a pastime that in spite of our thin veneer of culture and technology, we still indulge in today.

Nevertheless, through all the stages of human advancement, there exists this sensing of a higher presence that seems to be known as 'gods' and creators. Humans seem to have been borne to create. Again the question arises, who created our creators? On the ecclesiastical route we could ask, who, or what process was responsible for a 'divine god' who (we assume) was in existence before his great creational act? The teaching states, he was, is and always will be. It is possible, that the secret, without religious overtones, may simply be the original life from the waters belief, after all, there must be multitudes of earth-like worlds, in all that universal 'real estate', perhaps a world where evolution did succeed naturally and produced intelligent creatures that were the first and who eventually developed to the point of space travel. After discovering our world and seeing evolution struggling and failing, they began their great creational programme resulting finally with ourselves who will continue the process when we eventually find a suitable world at some point in the future. The ultimate secret of life must therefore be water, not only is it necessary for the continuance of life it is necessary for the commencement of it. It is said that, surgeons in the operating theatres and midwives often in the home, never get bored, accustomed to it, or indifferent about the birth process, they always remain to a certain extent overawed by it. One could watch a litter of cats being born and think little of it, but a cat will always exist as a cat and have little variation in its life and die as a cat. A human on the other hand could be looked at and cause one to wonder, will it become a great philosopher, an astronaut, a famous artist or poet? Or maybe a serial killer, murderous dictator? Such is the wonderment and the wide range of possible futures that await it in its development. More comfortable to imagine, it may stand on Mars one day, taking part in the process of a great terraforming operation when we take our inherited creative ability into the universe.

The Earth is the cradle of humanity but one doesn't live in the cradle forever. One of the astronauts on the Apollo programme, when out at the great rift of Hadley, on the moon, said "Man was born to explore and this is exploration at its greatest". We could add 'so far'. How many wonders await our discovery on future explorations beyond our solar system?

However, we must revisit the strange divergence of behaviour patterns in the human. The amazing capabilities on the one hand and the positivity evil and murderous thugs, drug dealers, the stabbings, the amazingly hateful and nasty things people are capable of saying to others in cowardly social media statements. Yet all these people can and do come together in armed forces and at certain points in time are able to kill and relish the act, in campaigns legally sanctioned by politicians enforcing their will in 'politics by other means', in short war but later, continuing on their positive and negative paths. Clearly, something failed, or went wrong in the creation of the human entity, which makes us even more curious about our creator(s) actual identity and heritage.

Noble attributes are desirable and necessary for humans to act in a positive manner and revive the destiny we were created for but evil and negative behaviour patterns are not, why therefore do they exist?

The greater achievements in science and space technology streak ahead of the more negative and evil human activity and religious beliefs accept that a divine god was responsible for them (a mystery in itself). But the Church was very responsible for a great subduing of advancement in the middle ages, particularly vulnerable, were the astronomers, who had to be very careful what they said and who they said it to in those times. Yet the strange paradox is, that the Church, itself more specifically, the Vatican, now has its own observatory and accepts the possibility of extra terrestrial life on other worlds, after all God is quite capable of populating some of them as well as Earth, but where is the 'heaven' they would ultimately go to? The Church has great wealth and a certain amount of power today, but it had even greater power and wealth in the dark ages and did not want to lose it, but even the Church was subject to a higher authority. Nevertheless, the Church could and did, condemn certain gifted and scientifically orientated individuals to death as heretics on the slightest pretext and viewed science as 'satanic' as it appeared to the Church and its dogmas. Gifted individuals of those times must have been immensely frustrated knowing that there was no mechanism in existence to develop and progress with their discoveries and this of course led to the so called 'Dark Ages' previously mentioned, that prevailed for so long awaiting more enlightened times. The Church was able to get away with these offences against science without fear, simply because any individual that had these talents was also looked on with suspicion by the current ruler, King Emperor or potentate, equally as much as the Church.

However, the Church remained subservient to the current Ruler, simply because Biblical writings and gospels that portrayed individuals that stepped outside the dutiful worship of a Ruler during his time were quickly condemned, such as Daniel. He was reported as being seen and heard worshipping a higher presence to the Ruler, Darius, who very quickly had him confined to the lion's den. Darius and his confidence must have suffered greatly, when learning that Daniel was saved from death by his god "And the Lord shut the lions' mouths".

Any passage in the Bible that seemed foreign and unacceptable to the King, such as where we mentioned in the work, that the angels may have tried to explain their origins and how they came to Earth from space would have been removed yet amazing accounts of the angels were left alone and not questioned at all, yet they clearly indicated a great power and influence over humanity. Perhaps more so than the Ruler, after all it would surely have been obvious to the Ruling Power that the angels made it clear in Genesis that it was they who created humans in the first place and not the king of kings.

The Ruler and all his courtiers and relations would be (indirectly) subservient to the angels and not a single and divine 'god' that they had always worshipped, therefore, other Beings claiming that they where the creators guiding humanity, would surely have seemed profoundly sacrilegious. Non-Christian lands and their Rulers had their own gods. But still believed in a greater place, Valhalla or a happy hunting ground 'wise' courtly advisors claimed, that the stars where just holes in the fabric of the firmament, where the heavenly light shone through, but a strong belief in a heaven and a divine creator prevailed.

Of course, all this would be in the 'post Moses era' and centuries later, at a period of the great thinkers and philosophers such as the ancient Greeks at their height of power, some, proclamations were being made regarding the universe, the shape of the Earth and scientifically accurate statements that were all disputed, derided and considered as heresy only a few centuries before our era.

PILLARS OF FIRE

So, how far have we come in establishing the actual identity, purpose and seemingly advanced creational and genetic capabilities of the angels? Well, strangely, after all the words, conjecture and assumptions in this and many other written works, the mental perception of the mysterious entities we call angels today, is just as strong as ever. This is probably due to a couple of factors. Firstly the limited number of people who study the Biblical accounts in detail in the Bible, particularly genesis and secondly, the enormous amount of people who see continually, the stereotype image of the angels on our Christmas cards.

Added to these factors are the quite familiar and often used expressions such as "She's a little angel and her expression is so angelic". Many a song writer has used in scores of love songs the word 'angel'. And so it seems that whatever is proposed regarding their real identity, purpose of profound connection with humanity, the accepted image of the angels remains unshakeable.

Many people habitually attend church every Sunday and consider themselves as religious, others eventually enter the priesthood and one assumes that coming to this point, it would become something of a shock to have this stereotype image of the angels shattered, as they would have to research intensely, as part of their theology study and training, all the details in Genesis described in this work, regarding the decidedly 'un-divine' nature and activity carried out by the angels.

As for the general public, when attending their weekly Sunday service, how many sermons, if any, have they been subjected to where the Priest has broached this obvious contrast in the two images pertaining to the angels? Having qualified and been ordained as priests, they must have been made aware of the startling alternative, as mentioned during their theological studies, why then are they so quiet about it? Is it fair to ignore it, when Moses himself described the negative actions of the angels as mentioned in this work? The priests and the clergymen must also be well aware of the plural expressions used in the creation event as "Let us" and "Make men in our image. Are they too controversial for any type of discussion, which seems, currently to be 'taboo' "?

We have to keep in mind of course, that although there are basic roots in similarity between the Jewish Faith, Christianity and Islam, over the centuries they have become distant from each other, yet revered the same patriarchs as Abraham and Moses. If one had a Catholic upbringing, there was a disturbing antagonism among Catholicism, that the Jews condemned Jesus, who was their Messiah, to death and still await the genuine Messiah, to them; Jesus was an imposter but even Pontius Pilate was reticent to crucify him and told the baying crowd "I need a crime, this man had done no wrong, he speaks of love and peace". As for the Catholic Faith and the Vatican when Nazis where escaping through the 'Odessa' network after the defeat of Germany, papers were processed by the Vatican, for them to be able to travel safely to foreign countries and the live there unmolested, perhaps because their original birth documents stated their religion as 'Catholic' which many of course oddly enough were. As for Islam it has to be said that a great distance now exists, in the practices of the extremists, their actions and beliefs, since the days of Abraham. Returning to the reticence to discuss the aforesaid, rather glaring differences between the perception of the angels and their activity, we must remember Moses, who wrote of the alleged factual activity of the angels, was a Jew himself and the Jews did consider themselves as a chosen people and the whole saga of exodus concerned the Hebrews. We needn't discuss the obvious animosity that still prevails today between the Hebrews and the Arabs that is the legacy of Moses Aaron and Joshua, in the friction between Israel and the Palestinians.

During the days of Moses and throughout the Old Testament, it seems strange that there was no analysis or discussions mentioned regarding the startling procedure of the angels method of departure. Many fell on their faces in awe and did not question it. Today, humans would most certainly question it. A questioning mind is responsible for all our studies, research scientific advances. When a rocket or a space shuttle took off, the people watched it in awe, until it was practically out of sight. After it had left the launch pad, they didn't simply walk away. So surely, it must have been the same for some of those who observed the rising of the angels. Their ascending, in the (mostly clear) blue skies of the Middle East would have been visible for thousands of feet before it went out of sight, unless of course the suspected 'manufactured' cloud hiding a structured craft was present. The power packs of the angels but have been quite small and blended in with their body form, unlike the rather cumbersome ones that are used today. This would not provoke any discussion of them by the patriarchs but their source of fuel must therefore have had limitations, they couldn't be climbing up to thousands of feet with their body becoming a pinpoint in the sky, therefore their objective must have been much lower hidden in a purposely manufactured 'cloud' but rarely as low as the one in Jacob's close encounter, when a stairway was lowered, so the angels could come down and go up without the use of their power source, but the cloud base (possibly again manufactured) would be very low. The patriarchs would not notice as much detail regarding the angels, simply because they may have felt it irreverent to stare and study them largely avoided this in a rather heads down attitude, much like the Jewish prisoners doing all that forced labour in work camps, such as Plaszów in Krakow when the immaculately uniformed SS guards strode in and selected out those to be killed, so room could be made for other Jews coming from other ghettos and closed down camps. We have mentioned that during all these horrors, not a single angel was in sight, to smite the oppressors of the Hebrews during all their suffering in World War Two.

In all my research and (one supposes) that of others, I never once encountered any written reference to 'wings' with regards to the angel's power source. Today, with the advantages of our awareness of modern day technology, astrophysics and genetic discoveries and capabilities medical science and so-forth, everything the angels accomplished, written about in such detail as genesis, has its modern day explanation, an explanation that is rather profound and worrisome with its implications for humanity, at some point in our future.

It has been calculated and demonstrated that the human body could never, in its current structure, have the muscles or muscle power to utilise wings as it is too heavy, even in the lightest human adult body, yet the angels where so human in appearance they could converse, eat and drink just like modern humans. It was the capabilities of the angels, as if 'rising in a flame' wasn't enough, they gave such technology and weaponry as the knowledge of destruction sound vibrations and a device so sophisticated, it augmented these vibrations immensely, served as a communication device to the 'gods' and of course its capability to destroy any potential enemy of the Hebrews, there are some quite pronounced and noticeable contradictions regarding the viewpoint on some of the issues mentioned in this work. We would mention the 'Eden' creation event. Eve, as the wife of Adam, gave birth to her sons as the first 'earth mother'. Science rejects the Biblical view of Genesis and the notion of 'Eve', yet state in their discoveries in genetics and human DNA that so called 'mitochondrial' DNA is only inherited from the female and in taking the process far back in time, we arrive at a point, of a single or first earthly mother, and who better to fit the description than Adam's wife Eve? Another contradiction is because of the vast distances between the stars, so distant that we have to use the term 'light years' that is a spacecraft travelling at 186,000 miles a second would take a full year to reach a solar system one light year away. Our nearest stellar neighbours are over four light years away. So at the moment interstellar travel is regarded as impossible. The contradiction is apparent, when science then goes on to mention the Einstein/Rosen Bridge theory of the possible existence of 'worm holes' in space and instead of spacecraft 'bee lining' on a straight course to its objective, it could utilise a 'bending' of space and time. One analogy used was to imagine a sheet of paper (say, A4 size) with a line written at the top of the page could be followed with a line at the bottom if we turn the page in cylinder fashion to join the top to the bottom, in other words, we have bent the fabric of space. Science accepts the possibility that life must exist in other words out in all those universal stars and planets, but baulk at the possibility that other world beings could have travelled to Earth in our past. At the pace of our own advancements, particularly from aeronautics to astronautics and contemplate that only a hundred and sixteen years have gone by from the Wright brothers to the Mars programme. Then imagine what advancements other living beings could have achieved a mere thousand years ahead of us. Maybe even many millions any theory discussed, and that maybe mathematically feasible, almost certainly one day will come to pass.

When we consider these factors, to presume that the theory of highly advanced beings came to Earth and genetically altered human DNA in order to advance human intelligence and creativity so not only far from science fiction, we are assured that it did happen and is already written down in the book that provides us with the clearest message that ET operated in Mesopotamia and in other parts of the World, that book is of course the Bible. It is not sacrilegious to say so, atheism is tolerable because people are not condemned to believe in a certain view point but are free to choose their beliefs, so it is, with any alternative theory that challenges the interpretation of the ecclesiastics, regarding the contents of the aforesaid book. Any righteous person would prefer the religious ideal to be true in all respects but is still free to think otherwise and point to some evidence of it. We have stated the word 'angel' in Hebrew simply means messenger and those beings amply fulfilled that role. The Greek word "Angoulos' means 'intermediary'. Even the word 'giant' is said to simply mean having great capabilities, they were the offspring of the gods that "came into the daughter of man" etc. But seemingly did not fulfil the objectives assigned to them and turned out Brutish.

It seems rather hypocritical to state that a higher intelligence could not have manipulated human DNA; when we ourselves are doing exactly the same thing, except of course, where the identity of the creature (or subject) has changed. In our case, it is the current operation already underway, to create (or re-create) the woolly mammoths.

Extremely fresh samples of their well-preserved DNA have been obtained from the Siberian wastes. A string of their DNA known as the Double Helix, rather like a twisted ladder, could be drawn out, with 'rungs' containing the blueprint for the creatures bodily aspects and metabolism. By snipping a section out and inserting different portion, perhaps from an elephant, their modern counterpart, that hope is, that they could recreate the mammoth creatures in some kind of Jurassic park experiment. The area where they could freely roam has already been earmarked.

Here, we have a scenario where living creatures (ourselves) manipulating the woolly mammoths DNA, to bring it forward thousands of years. Does this not exactly mirror the theory of "another world' intelligence, long in our past carrying out the same process on a pre-human, to bring it forward in time? An enormous amount of evolutionary time that would have been necessary for it to evolve. A creature that had suitable bodily characteristics that could be enhanced. In particular the human brain, remembering that we ourselves have discovered a gene said to control intelligence. Such hypothetical ETs could have extracted certain cellular material from a pre-human entity and inserted other material that would assure the development of its creative abilities but also manipulated other experimental failures such as Neanderthal to extinction. As we have said it did degenerate and retrogress, as is evident in the fossil record and so the hypothetical ET entities, brought about a giant leap forward in excruciatingly slow creeping evolutionary time, enter the 'Cro-Magnon' our only acceptable predecessors.

However, even Cro-Magnon, although viewed as a major success in their manipulations, it has been suggested that normal evolutionary processes from that period on, took on two diversionary paths. The savage and evil tendencies and metal aberrations slowly began to appear and prevail, even to this day. Conversely, on the righteous path, we have the patriarchs and saints and enlightened ones, some of whom risked and indeed sacrificed their own lives to preach the positive and desirable traits and commandments given to humans by our alleged ETs, for all to obey. These inspired individuals knew there was a greater power than any earthly living creature and interpreted it in the way humans mostly believe today, in their religious practices. On this positive track, the great thinkers, designers, mathematicians of the Egyptian civilisation (again interpreting the higher power in their own way) appeared, then the great thinkers and philosophers of the Greek culture whose pronouncements regarding the Earth and the Universe, where so accurate for their time. Bruno, Galileo, Leonard-de-Vinci, Newton, Einstein and the physicists and astronomers, the great brains of NASA that have put humans on their (one might say) inevitable path to (return) to the stars.

Perhaps the only negative feature in all of this is that great men of science can also be, to an extent, 'closed minded'. The old adage rises here, "if a scientist suggests that a certain thing will be possible in the future. He is probably right, but if he states out of the question or impossible, he is almost certainly wrong".

After a thorough examination of the discovery in recent times, of the 'Hitler Diaries' they were pronounced as genuine but later they where proved to be fakes. The famous author, Sir Arthur Conan Doyle, believed whole heartedly in the photography of the 'Cottingley Fairies', that two young girls had cut out of a book and photographed dancing among the flowers. Later in life one of the girls admitted on her deathbed that they had faked the whole thing using a Box Brownie to take the photographs. On another occasion a famous art critic stood back in awe when assessing a work of art painted in a garish 'modern art' style and stated he could see the hidden meaning that the artist was trying to portray. One can imagine his feelings when told a chimpanzee had been given a brush and some paint and occasionally walked across it, as the canvas lay on the floor covered with various colours splurged on it by the chimp. Clearly 'experts' and scientists are not infallible beings.

Regarding the theory that the Biblical angels where responsible, being 'not of this earth' for human creation and development, there exists an alternative suggestion that it was not manipulation of genes that caused the great surge of intelligence and brain development in the human but rather the 'rewiring' of the brain by purposeful action. Cases are on record where humans, after a fall and suffering head trauma, began to develop talents they never before had, such as becoming highly proficient pianist or developing a flair for mathematics. All this success that the blow on the head caused some neurological circuit to 'bridge' so to speak, indicating that if our neurosurgeons identified which circuits in the brain were responsible for certain talents and abilities then it may be possible to carry out an operation rather like re-wiring a computer. The brain of Einstein has been preserved and sliced into segments and then sent to various institutions that all agreed that his brain was wired differently than the average human.

In this work, we highlighted the longevity of the patriarchs, spoken so 'matter-of-factly' in the Book of Genesis regarding the antediluvian people and why, after Noah, who was clearly endowed with this trait there was incredible demise in the average human in terms of lifespan? However, a graph clearly shows that human longevity is rising, not in a rising and falling mode but a fairly straight line. Of course fluctuations would have been noticed in the past if such analysis had taken place, wars, pestilences and plagues, the ravages of Spanish flu, caused the deaths of so many in the early part of the twentieth century, and of course all the vast decimation of the First World War on both sides in terms of human lives. It would seem unlikely that there is a single gene responsible for longevity as so many other factors influence it. General health, a more polluted environment compared to a fresh air or farming and outdoor agricultural occupations. But as regards to general longevity all the genes in our metabolism will almost certainly be discovered and isolated and together with stem cells and their applications, the utopian idea of a perfect race may be achieved in the passage of time.

It may be possible by identifying the genes and the process that occurs in the womb, pertaining to the development of the arms and legs of the foetus being formed, that we may be able to gain control of the ability to regenerate or re-grow an arm or leg lost in war or an accident. At the current rate of scientific advancement in this field, anything is possible. The prosthetic limb manufacturing industry, which in itself is so advanced and helpful to many today, would become redundant tomorrow. It may be possible to genetically regrow an eye and our vital organs already as stated to be quite feasible according to the American Institution for the Advancement of Science.

If any of this ever comes to pass, one would hope and expect that the highest priority would be given the identification of the negative genes, that are part of our savage past and continual aggressive behaviour with violent crime and man's inhumanity to man. Most of all the elimination of the negative forces that cause the human to abdicate from all human rational behaviour in our incessant wars and conflicts, and the urge to continually destroy each other in such actions.

A relevant feature of this type of negativity is the fact the first consideration of any new invention is its analysis with regard to capability and usefulness as an advantageous war weapon or application in support of such.

Conspiracy theories currently in Vogue have it, that a scientifically developed site in Alaska, initially non-secret and publically available for inspection, was intended for positive weather control in order to relieve drought stricken areas for example. It was a process that beamed high power electronic forces into the high atmosphere, now it is a highly secret and off limits military establishment, possibly used for manipulation of the weather patterns and its destructive forces, the jet stream and the so-called El Nino, plus lightning strikes under control and aimed possibly at the enemy weapon establishments. The ability to cause floods and bog down enemy forces. For all we know it may already be under functional testing as freak weather conditions seem to be more prevalent today. A 70° temperature in February 2019 in parts of Britain for example, said to be caused by a southerly dip in the jet stream. It is securely located in a fairly remote area easy to protect and guard. Of course it could still be manipulated for positive and helpful purposes, if the Military allowed it. Currently it is said that the US had spent more money than it can hide on so called black projects in most fields of defence and military research. In the past, the jet stream was used by many a commercial airline to utilise, and if they were on that compass heading the aircraft could throttle back and utilise its additional speed in order to save fuel. Now it appears to be more erratic.

Human advancement seems to be somewhat retarded by these negative and warlike actions that are firmly loaded in our mental makeup.

Although the Catholic Church views the Pope as infallible, he would be gracious enough to admit that he is not. No human is, or ever will be infallible. Recently, a cardinal was indicted for paedophile activity. Cardinals eventually get elected as Popes.

PILLARS OF FIRE

It is debatable whether our alleged creative ETs (or angels) made some errors in the assumed process of human mental manipulating. Where they actually intent on producing a faultless functioning and advanced human? Or where they satisfied with that they had achieved? Which, it must be said, is quite substantive? In any case, they could hardly be described as only behaving in an 'angelic' way, when we consider the directives that were given to Moses after the exodus from Egypt and the most savage slaughtering of the Assyrians during the night as the Hebrews slept, carried out by the angels themselves.

To return again to the frequently used term "let us go down" that features so often in their operation is with the 'possibly hybrid' people we know as the patriarchs.

The patriarchs would be well aware that they would have to come down, as they had observed them arising on their pillars of fire so often. We suggested the possibility of a 'cloud' being purposely generated to hide their assumed structured craft, simply because the angels had to stop somewhere not too far above the Earth. After all the angels did admit this method of disguising their craft when stating to Moses "I come to thee in a thick cloud", prior to their landing on Mount Sinai.

However, their craft would not be permanently in the hover mode in a cloud, but only when the angels had the need to rise or descend, and no doubt landed on the tops of the high mountain. This would have been to keep well away from human eyes. It was feasible then as no mountaineers or climbing organisations existed in Biblical times, which was probably a good thing as any that reached the top may have been 'shot through' as was clearly explained to Moses before he ascended Mount Sinai for the receipt of the tablets that contained human behaviour orders, lasered into the stones. They were commands not advice, as the orders all began with the words "thou shalt not".

Nowadays, of course, the mountain tops have all mostly been denied to them that is, assuming they still need them which is doubtful, as humans have scaled even the highest of them.

In my manuscript 'when the moon came' dealing with lunar mysteries and a seemingly ET presence there, the moon would have been a safe and convenient location for them, particularly as having the added advantage of one side continually facing Earth, in order to keep an eye on their human creations. But now, we push back their frontiers even further by our frequent visits there during the Apollo programme. During the astronaut's visits there, they observed UFO's Buzzing their aircraft moving ahead of them and trailing them. Photographs of objects orbiting the moon where taken from the command module in close proximity to the moon.

PILLARS OF FIRE

It remains doubtful that we caused them to abandon the moon altogether because their suspected mining of surface material seems to be still taking place, also the T.L.P. or trans lunar phenomena of moving white and coloured lights, even an intense ruby red light in a crater, still prevails, also, they would be aware that humans have not transversed the moon but confined their activities and sample gathering to only a few areas. In any case, alleged ETs could freely operate on the dark side, as they seem to have extremely bright sources of light at their disposal.

Another safe location for them could be within the Earth itself. Certain factors seem to support this hollow Earth theory. In the past some of the information gathering probes sent directly over the pole, were lost, while other probes in Northern areas not traversing the pole where retrieved. UFOs are often seen heading on a northerly course. Earthly satellites sent up by the European Space Agency have photographed a hole or dark depression at the pole. Arctic explorers put it on record; (those that have gone the extra mile and not planted the flag as soon as the compass needle pointed down) noticed the horizon foreshortening, as though they were approaching the rim. Furthermore, explorers have noticed a distinct rise in temperature on these occasions and also 'bloom mats' of varying colours on the surface of the snow, as though the pollen like material was blowing up from the hole.

We have said that Genesis, in particular 'Exodus' concentrated on the operation that seemed like a population dispersal mission and only appeared to concern the Hebrews, but other operations would have been in progress with other groups of 'angels' working on amazing stone structures to suit their own purpose at the time. A 'building site' in Pumapunku in Bolivia is absolutely stunning. No ancient humans could have cut all the amazingly precise recesses, joints and angles so smoothly and accurately cut and formed without any advanced cutting equipment, noticeable, even in the blocks themselves. Another example of this advanced technology is Tiahuanaco in South America. As well as manipulating human DNA, they may well have involved themselves in experiments with other earthly creatures. We mentioned briefly, the horse, an animal that has been the most useful and most utilised creature by humans ever since it was first tamed. It has served humans for at least a couple of millennia. It has been exploited for its great strength in agriculture, trained and used by humans in warfare.

In peace, its ability to transport humans great distances was obvious. Finally after all its help when aged and no longer able to fulfil its various roles it could be eaten. A sad end for such a noble animal. Anthropologists tell us that in its early evolutionary period it was not much bigger than a good sized dog. Evolution with regard to all life forms and growths is incredibly slow (apart from human emergence). It does not change for changes sake and there was no natural reason for it to multiply in size to around three or four times its volume in regard to the horse. This begs the question of course, could it also have been genetically manipulated in order to assist the early humans in their farming and transport requirements? If alleged ET creators could achieve such success in human development, manipulating the genes of animals may not have been a problem for them. We also mentioned in the text, when dealing with their alleged creative operations in their chosen garden of Eden zone by the assumed ETs (A.K.A angels) that after Adam was created, he appeared to be unaware of other earthly creatures as the Biblical text states, that the creator(s) brought animals of varying types to Adam in order for him to name them and as he did so "That was the name thereof".

It would make sense if Adam was still on the 'learning mode' and within the confines of the garden and had not yet been released to "till the Earth and go forth and multiply" etc., that he would be aware of other earthly creatures. The dinosaur had long gone but the primates had flourished over (we are told) for fifty million years and the Earth would have been a 'planet of the apes'. In any case, Adam owed his very existence to a type of primate in order to fit in with the angel's creative activity with regard to producing an advanced intelligently enhanced being.

However, we must ask, how many other life forms of the edible variety, existed on Earth at the time? Such as cows, sheep, pigs, goats etc. Although the Biblical texts seem to suggest that humans should be vegetarians, the animals that "went in, two by two" into the ark would certainly, in some of their number been of the edible type.

The question now arises, where the animal species brought to Adam to name, of earthly origin or creatures that had evolved on the creator's home planet? It was mentioned in the Biblical account, that creatures would remain "each unto their kind". There is a very distinct lack of transitional species in order to conform to the established evolutionary process going back into the mists of time. Furthermore as we have said their DNA profile and chromosome pattern ensures they remain 'each unto their kind' and cannot cross breed with other earthly creatures.

It is hardly likely that alleged ETs would bring live creatures to Earth but samples of their DNA profiles could be brought in great numbers and introduced to Earth, just as humans, long into the future may do, if and when we terraform other planets in our own system or perhaps another, as earth like worlds seem to be continually discovered situated within the ideal place in their solar system. And in any case our sun's life is finite and such an exodus, if possible, at the time would have to occur to ensure the survival of our species.

So it would make sense if the animals DNA profiles were brought to Earth and nurtured into existence during the same period the ETs where manipulating a suitable primate candidate. The animals would have developed and procreated to the forms brought to Adam. The alleged 'operators' would have been reluctant to inform Adam of the long list of ET names of each animal and thought it a better idea to let him name them as that way, he would remember them more easily.

When we speak of DNA profiles being nurtured and frozen for whatever reason, it is a fact that a specific building is already established and functioning, to preserve in cold storage, the DNA of all the foliage and fauna that exists on Earth today as part of the preparation for a catastrophic elimination event where an asteroid may strike the Earth and obviously would destroy many living and growing species. It is situated in Spitsbergen in Norway. It could be called a 'doomsday vault' or fit the description of a modern day ark. It is built to be virtually indestructible. In such a catastrophic event there would always be human survivors. Clearly the purpose of such an establishment would be the hope that the Earth after a post 'apocalypse' period could with time be restored to its former glory. We regard to survivors, there would have been advanced warning due to the sky watch programme already established, that monitor the largest and most threatening objects that could endanger the Earth in their orbits, particularly if deflected only slightly in their course. Such objects can be monitored from vast distances from Earth and just like a few films that have been made regarding an 'E.L.E. Event', a selection process, with regard to humans would be implemented (and probably has). In cold logical terms, it may seem this makes very good sense.

Alarmingly, in the past these objects have approached the Earth in a rather sneaky fashion, from behind the sun for instance and only detected when moving away from the Earth.

Asteroids have actually passed between the moon and the Earth. It's pretty certain that they would have been observed from a great distance away and to eventually pass so close to earth would, in calculations when initially observed seem almost certainly be on collision course with Earth simply because, in astronomical terms we could almost reach out and touch it. Yet we were not told this. Of course all that DNA could also be installed in a departing spacecraft from Earth . The Spitsbergen unit has pullout drawers, rather like those seen in a natural history museum, that when pulled out show insects and Butterflies and so forth in their thousands.

When we mentioned, that the astronomers may have detected a possible impact event, but there was a chance in place, that it could miss, the General Public would not be informed. Cold hard decisions would have to be made and the consideration would certainly be raised, that many casualties would occur due to panic. Looting and chaos would reign, so there would not be a general release of the danger to the general public, if this scenario could be avoided. From all that we have said regarding the possible creation event regarding humans, the ETs (accepted in Biblical times as 'angels') would be aware their identity is safe. If their existence is known in high places modern day humans could not be trusted to be made aware of it. Today, they only move around the Earth in their modern day operations in what we call the UFO phenomena but still interact with humanity and after all their current advancement since their initial creation programme carried out by their predecessors, they could surely be able to protect the Earth very easily from any aforementioned E.L.E. Event but would they? Given our own earthly 'subduing' carried out all over the world but not in, the way intended by the original creators, we seem more intent on pillaging of the world's resources and in this situation we may only exist by kind permission of the ET creators. On the other hand, if a divine heavenly god did create the Earth and man by waiving an airy hand, we asked, would a similar action rid us of the celestial threat to his creations and their earthly habitat by any approaching orbit debris? ET creators, having gone to so much trouble to produce ourselves, would also, we assume not wish to have it all destroyed, so it seems (looking on the positive side) we have a double protection insurance. Financial costs always rears its ugly head and although many and varied methods to deflect N.E.Os or near Earth objects, away from the Earth, have been suggested and deemed feasible, how much expenditure has actually been allocated to implement such a procedure? After all, vast sums are said to be sanctioned for the aforementioned black projects. If alleged creative ETs did exist at the time of Noah and it was not a human elimination event decided by them to flood the Earth, then it mirrors the same scenario previously mentioned, regarding the best of the crop so to speak being pre-selected and also the animal pairs for later procreation.

At that time, the ETs may not have had the power to deal with any approaching celestial threat and if a large asteroid was heading for the middle of the Pacific or the Atlantic Ocean, one can only imagine the devastation in terms of the subsequent flooding, such an event would cause.

However, we must recall the statements made in this work after the event that is mentioned on page 34, "A wind was 'made' to pass over the earth and the waters assuaged. The fountains of the deep and the windows of heaven where <u>stopped</u> and the rain from Heaven restrained etc., so, even if the angels did not instigate the flood, it is clear that they had the power to stop it.

It is said that twelve hundred other earthly cultures have specific flood legends. The majority of the Earth's surface is water and the remaining land areas have seventy five percent of sedimentary layers. Many areas once above land are now beneath the sea, with many still being discovered so almost all of the Earth has sedimentary layers of alluvial deposits (i.e. flooding).

So where are our hypothetical creators now? We know that they are coursing through our skies in the UFO phenomena, but having completed their earthly creative mission they still maintain an interest in the huge amount of generations that have passed since their halcyon days in the Garden of Eden. This is evident in the continuing amount of alleged abductions that are said to be in their thousands. Naturally, they would be aware that they had not achieved perfection when we mentioned the more negative pursuits and pastimes so why have they allowed such a long time to pass when earlier, they could have intervened when war and conflict was more predominant that it is today? The answer must be, that with all the alleged abductions involving the removal and study of human DNA and metabolism that the human brain is slowly righting itself and in time the positive genes will prevail. Perhaps finally, the excess brain material we have been given that so defies the accepted evolutionary theory, is at last stirring itself. After initial arrival of alleged ET 'creators', although needing an enormous amount of time to assess and study a world teeming with life of all descriptions, they must have also thoroughly surveyed our solar system.

We have mentioned possible ET habitats established within the Earth or under its seas and also on and possibly within the moon. They may well be responsible for all the translunar phenomena we know as T.L.P. regarding moving lights, many of which have been observed by professional and amateur astronomers, and with our current roving vehicles, strange things are continually reported. A Martian probe detected methane a certain signature of life. People, cows and cattle emit it all the time. But it also is released by volcanoes. At one point in its existence, mars had very prolific volcanic activity. Olympus Mons is the biggest volcano on any other planet that we know of in our solar system but they are inactive and seismologically quiet today. So what is emitting the methane? If there are living creatures under the Martian surface (which needn't be humanoid), their methane emissions would eventually reach the surface or possibly physically piped to the surface in the case of any intelligent beings. Clearly our initial 'creators' or ETs should obviously have the ability to streak around our solar system with ease, since being able to travel to Earth in the first place and would know our solar system far better than we do ourselves. As said helium three is a very valuable commodity as a power source for hypothetical ETs and it is apparently in abundance on the moon.

If we accept that ETs found Earth and went about the process of enhancing human evolution, they must have had the ability to assess and study the universe and have been able to decide the most likely direction to travel. This seems to indicate that our type of star would be the type judged as the best candidate for the development of life in any attendant planet that may exist in the 'goldilocks' zone (no extremes either way in temperature) yet the sun is not as stable as we would like it to be. It goes through a 'sun spot' cycle of around eleven years. It is capable of violent outbursts of radiation that can cause havoc on and around the Earth that can affect the electronic equipment in our orbiting satellites and affect the orbiting space station. These bursts can also knock out the power grid. A good example of this was an event in the 1970s when a large tract of land was affected from northeast Canada and into the USA. Such burst can, it is said, temporarily 'inflate' the atmosphere and introduce atmospheric particles to a higher level, thereby slowing down through friction any lower orbiting satellites which then having been retarded in their velocity begin to slowly spiral into the atmosphere and burn up.

ETs prior travelling to Earth would or should be well aware of these activities and if they were capable of interstellar travel, then their ability to study and analyse stars must have decided our type of star was the best candidate to contain the type of planet they were looking for before their arrival. The strange paradox exists, that our astronomers, who must believe our category of star is an ideal subject for planetary life, given the abundance on it, that exists on Earth, state that with our own research and astronomical search of the universe in our S.E.T.I. Programme that the category of small orange stars may be the best place to look for evidence of extra terrestrial life. They say K-stars that are smaller and cooler than the sun, could provide the perfect conditions for exoplanets to host life. This is according to NASA scientist Glada Arney.

Our sun is of the type that shines for ten billion years and it is already middle-aged. Said to be 4.5 billion years old, but these K-type stars are said to shine for at least fifteen billion years, while not exhibiting the aforementioned extreme activity that could disrupt life. Our life would be well disrupted or may even not exist if it were not for our magnetic field that deflects most of the 'solar wind' around and away from our atmosphere, otherwise we would die of radiation poisoning. Dr. Arney goes on to say "The temperature of K-stars stays steady", she tell us that Red Dwarfs known as "M" type stars, the temperature fluctuates, but 'K' type stars are in a 'sweet spot' and any planets circling them would be the best place to look for signs of life or 'bio-signatures' i.e. methane for example. However, would not our assumed ET creators already have done this kind of analysis long ago? Maybe even visited them and discarded them as havens? All our pronouncements made today, during this life search, may have been done thousands of years ago, and certainly points out how rare life giving planets are, and gives rise to the question are we the first?

Of course if the E.T.H. is evident on our world (extra terrestrial hypothesis), clearly we are not the first. It is also possible that they may have had nothing to do with our creation and would have been attracted to our world because of our sun's cosmic signature. If ETs are here, as millennia of evidence suggests they are certainly in no hurry to leave. In any event none of this is any help in resolving the mystery or our own human origins.

In this matter, when we spoke of all the time spent on chimpanzees to 'humanise them', their basic lack of intelligence prevents them exceeding a certain maxim. Yet because of the unresolved issue of human evolvement, they will always be attended to as the last chance to reinforce the Darwinian Ideal.

We have mentioned the intelligence of dogs for example, in comparison to our alleged 'cousins' the chimpanzees. An amazing account in the newspaper 'Metro' (March 14th 2019) described a Labrador, known as an 'assistance dog' and how it helps a disabled woman with chores around the house, fetches food from the fridge etc. Although disabled, the lady married and the dog 'Ethan' was the ring bearer. It can even make contactless payments for the lady at the supermarket. He goes into the ladies bag, finds her payment card, she says "touch" and the dog presents the card in its teeth and waits for the 'beep'. He even waits for the receipt and gently tears it off. Amazing canine intelligence.

It is a strange paradox that so many other earthly creatures can display such evidence of intelligence, when one would naturally expect our alleged cousins to even more astounding things.

If our hypothetical 'creators' ever reveal themselves to us it would be for a very good reason. One very good reason for them not to and they would know it, would be their knowledge that even if they previously informed the Whitehouse Staff that they would shortly land on the Whitehouse lawn, as soon as they touched down their craft would be immediately surrounded with soldiers, bristling with weapons and cocked machine guns, one false move would be all that was needed for the trigger happy soldiers, soaked in such scenarios in films, would always assume, because of their human inbred fears lodged in the brain, that something unknown was a threat.

Many people believe, for all that, in a suggestion that such contact has already been made and that certain highly placed individuals and scientists are working with ETs and making deals with them.

'Their technology' for our co-operation with them'. Even suggesting that the US Sanctions some of the abduction cases after all it is rare that the abductees never return. They do, even if it's after a couple of days. The mystery of the cattle mutilations and their neatly incised organ removal and blood draining process is always attributed to ETs but black helicopters are nearly always nearby at some point. It has even been stated by a high ranking officer, after retiring, stated (with regard to area 51) we've got stuff out there fifty years ahead of any other country. In this country, people retire from the armed forces have to sign 'The Official Secrets Act', not to disclose any sensitive information they possess and it is the same, as far as I am aware, for US Service people. In their operations of course, we don't know if these kinds of statements are intended to be released in this so-called black propaganda. Any enemy considering a sneak attack may well think twice about it when learning of such statements.

We know of course, and are aware, that it is unwise to take everything we read or see on the internet and fake news is very much in vogue at the moment, but when TV programmes appear that portray such things in the ancient aliens genre, we assume that some research has taken place in order to substantiate the story.

One such place was mentioned as Dulce in New Mexico (there is always someone who has been there and seen it) the individuals stated on the TV programme that during a tunnelling programme an accidental breakthrough occurred to a multi-layers research centre, where humans where working alongside aliens. Before barely escaping with his life, he noticed what appeared to be a series of foetuses in some kind of jars containing blush liquid. If this is beginning to sound familiar, it is because we mentioned this when commenting on what the alleged female abductees had reported when hypnotically regressed to release details of what they went through during their experience of, and observations, in the craft. If it is happening in various parts of the world and possibly in the UFOs mother ships, an awful lot of emerging alien beings are currently being produced, or have already been produced for some clear purpose. Some of these alleged events in abduction cases were reported decades ago.

We have two theories to examine if it is really happening, in the first instance, with regards to the ET creation scenario of humanity. We speculated on how the alleged ETs would view our current behaviour patterns, for which their predecessors where responsible and now their successors (today's ETs) have inherited the responsibility from their forebears whether they like it or not.

We could take the view that all these ET hybrids will eventually be released when mature and fully trained and briefed on their procedures during their future earthly role, will be free of all negative genes and act, lead by example, and perhaps having high intelligence obtain as many high positions as possible in the military and in politics and eventually breeding out all the negativity displayed in current human behaviour.

In this scenario, we would have to comment, that if that alleged ETs are the original creators of humanity, that is, the creation of the only successful human ancestor the Cro-Magnon peoples, then it has taken fifty (maybe) a hundred thousand years for them to decide on this so-called hybrid insertion programme.

The indications are that this theory is most unlikely and there is another purpose altogether for all these hybrid creations. This brings us to the second theory or possibility for this multitude of hybrids.

When they completed their final successful creation, that is, the aforementioned Aurignacion or Cro-Magnon peoples they were quite satisfied with their results and did not attach too much importance to the obvious negative factors displayed along with the positive, when observing human behaviour. The reason for this was perhaps that they fully expected it and in this regard took steps to cater for it by bestowing all that additional brain material in the human skull that is unexplainable in natural selection and the normal evolutionary terms this is because these natural evolutionary processes never over endow any species in advance of its needs to survive.

Highly advanced ET creators who maybe expertly proficient in the manipulation of any earthly life forms, could possibly 'over endow' any creature they saw fit. We could quote a previous example of this with referring back to our comments on the convenient development of the horse perhaps ET 'over endowed' that lifeform with extra growth and stature hormones. It doesn't seem likely that natural selection would do so. However, to continue with the analysis of this second theory, if humanity were created as theorised by ET genetic creation, and it took place in the most distance period possible for the appearance of Cro-Magnum, that is, a hundred thousand years ago, then the alleged ETs had produced a creature that a hundred thousand years later began completing plans to travel to mars, that is underway today. But the case, that the hypothetical ET creators have, for all we know, more than a million years of evolution behind them, what could they have achieved in all that time? It's dangerous to say so, but the possibility that they are (or were) inter-galactic travellers is most unlikely. In any case there is quite sufficient real estate to look over with the estimated number of stars (being around a hundred billion) in our galaxy alone. As for the planets, we could multiply the hundred billion by five, maybe even ten, for the amount of possible planets, with such surmised length evolution behind them, not to mention the additional one hundred thousand years since their hypothetical earthly creation mission. They may have achieved all they ever wished to and there could be little else to learn. In short, they may have begun to atrophy in thought and deed and need a completely new and invigorating process to prevent the possibility of their evolution coming to an end.

We now have a completely different theory regarding the alleged foetuses reportedly seen so many times. Their human creations could now be serving them in all those countless abduction claims. In one convincing case, a lady under hypnotic regression, to analyse her claims that she had been abducted several times and the ETs always knew where to find their victims as in each case a tiny communication device had been inserted somewhere in the body. She related a rather astounding scenario where she went through an alleged 'bonding' process with an attractive child that clearly was not 100% human but had reached the age of a toddler she seemed to sense the child was or at least partly hers. Countless numbers of these alleged hybrids could have been transported back to their home planet to possibly invigorate their race. It is said that the blood of cattle is the most similar to human blood. Is there any connection with the so-called cattle mutilations that occur so often in the American West in the cattle rearing ranches? They are not in fact 'mutilations' as per the usual meaning of the term, but surgical operations of a precise nature. However, they have one thing in common, a complete absence of blood in the animal.

Quite often before or after a discovery of these carcases, black helicopters are frequently seen. This would tend to reinforce the claims that humans are working with ETs and condone these operations in return for ET technology. Suddenly a host of new discoveries of a highly technical nature all appearing together in abundance and not in the usual way, in this case, it would not be surprising to have someone state that the US had craft at least fifty years ahead of any other nation.

This second theory appears more acceptable than imaginative science fiction when we reflect on the present of ETs in Earth space ever since the 'aliens of Abraham'. If such a process just evaluated is, occurring ETs would not be in a hurry to leave a word that is actively invigorating them and their own world's population. Perhaps one day we will meet them or they us. What a TV programme that would be for 'meet the ancestors'.

In this regard, clearly, humans need not fear them but they would most certainly fear us and be glad of the US military in assisting them in some alien pre-arranged deal.

With regard to the frequently reported UFO crashes, it always seems that trained recovery teams usually military, yet displaying no insignia, quickly turn up, indicating a fully trained recovery team on permanent alert ready and waiting to rapidly travel to and cordon off crash sites and usher everyone out of the area, then pick up and transport the craft away, either by helicopter or flat bed transporter.

With regard to the craft, they are almost certainly earthly machines, although possibly 'reverse engineered' from actual alien craft. If ET has been in earth space as long as hypothesised at least one or two must have come to grief sometime and if it was in the USA, then they certainly have the edge in terms of advanced ET technology. Perhaps the well-known Roswell incident is genuine but as for the rest, mentioned in all those other events it would be quite ludicrous to expect ET advanced space craft that had the ability to travel the galaxy only to come to grief on Earth so regularly.

Of course, there is the theory that the craft meeting their end, are nothing to do with ET at all, but are the result of captured Nazi technology. In 'Operation Paperclip' at the close of the war, the US got the pick of the crop of the Nazi scientists, such as Werner Von Braun who naturally preferred to surrender to the allies rather than the Russians. This is not surprising when considering all the atrocities committed by the Nazis in their Russian campaigns. Christopher Columbus collected many ancient maps and knew about the circular shape of the Earth the most intriguing of all was the so-called 'Piri Reis' chart that seemed to have been compiled as though from the air but most amazingly showed every cove and inlet in the Antarctic now under a mile or ice. It would have had to have been compiled thousands of years ago when Antarctic zones where ice free. The map agreed with the comparatively recent sonar sounding that enabled cartographers to detail all coves and inlets featured on the map, and they matched exactly.

The Nazca Plain in Peru is interesting and also, can only be appreciated from the air when aircraft flew over it. Vehicles travelled across the highway through it for years without even knowing the huge drawing and the many straight lines depicted were there.

Many amazing objects have been found indicating ancient advanced technology; in particular an ancient computer discovered by Greek sponge divers near the island of Antikythera in 1900 and was about the size of a portable typewriter. It had numerous cogs and wheels all intermeshing like a clock. It must have been cleverly designed for some advanced purpose with a watchmaker's tools and skills.

However, whenever we encounter ooparts or artifacts out of their time, the temptation always exists to assign them to 'ancient astronauts' rather than enlightened humans, but the deeper question is how did all those ancient humans acquire such wisdom and creativity in the first place? Here the theory covered in this work once more arises, and steps in with the answer Andrew Tomas, in his book 'We are not the First' (sphere) has a section titled "they conquered space long before we did".

He had it that mans desire to fly not only in the air but also amidst the stars, was present in ancient times. He quotes from the 4,700 year old Babylonian Epic of the Etana when he allegedly had a flight that lasted for an hour at first, then for three hours. Etana was instructed to look down, and he described the Earth, as we knew it looks, from a great height. After the third hour, the Earth was described as a 'speck', which would have to be far out in space.

Anu was described as a god of "The Heavenly great depths". In short outer space. An extract from the Egyptian book of the dead, over 3,500 years old reads "this place has no air, its depth is unfathomable and it is black as the blackest night" where could this possibly be but outer space?

We mentioned in the work that the Bible and its scriptures where frequently altered or taken out completely in some cases. An example is The Book of Enoch that contains similar quotes. The Book of Enoch was rejected by the Bishops and Rabbis. However, it was found to be incorporated in the Dead Sea Scrolls that could be said to be the oldest Bible in the World, going back to the second century BC. Some extracts say "And they lifted me up into Heaven" (who are 'they') "And it was hot as fire and cold as ice". "I saw the places of the luminaries". These are amazingly accurate statements if they are nothing but guess work. Our hypothetical creators as a diversion from their main objectives seem quite happy to have been running an excursion service for their chosen ones. I think the most profound quotation comes from the second century of our era. Lucian, a Greek author, wrote a novel *Vera Historia*. In it he describes a voyage that almost mirrors the voyage of Apollo 8 the first mission to leave Earth orbit and circle the moon.

"Having thus continued our course through the sky for the space of seven days, on the eighth day we encountered a sort of Earth in the air resembling a large shining circular island spreading a remarkably brilliant light around it".

How can we explain accounts such as these in a rational manner? Well, in a sense, if the amazing human creation event did take place with beings arriving on Earth to enhance intelligence in a suitable recipient, the intelligent being so produced would be rather like children in a stable home or environment looking up to their parents in awe and viewed them with great respect as they seemed so clever and wise and the children would obey them, learn from them without question. They would be open and quite receptive to learn about the World all around them and would absorb in a natural manner much detail, and at some point their parents would answer the usual questions asked about where they came from. Although some parents avoid this issue through embarrassment and leave it to the school to give them tuition in the sex lessons they receive, creative other world ETs would make it all very clear to them and would expect them to now have complete access to the tree of knowledge their ancestors raided so disobediently before the other world tutors where finished assessing their capabilities. Humans, at this point would be receiving the first mental inputs that gradually became legends that they were first created by 'gods from the sky' and this belief spread far and wide as humans also did around the world. As part of their tuition, the creators would make their creations aware of the nature of their environment and the world in its place in the firmament.

PILLARS OF FIRE

The wisest of their creations would be taken into space, shown how eventually they themselves would be expected to achieve such things and put them on the road to finally attain, over the millennia, the abilities to create and indeed become as the 'gods' themselves.

Humans following this pattern the more enlightened ones go onto higher education, join universities, become tutors and professors, teach astronomy, coach astrophysics. Become astronauts, long to find and colonise other worlds and mentally follow the process without realising that they are 'programmed' to do just that, back in the mists of time, when the necessary intelligent genes were being installed in their distance predecessors in the establishment on Earth that we know as 'Eden'.

We have mentioned more than once, that human negativity exists alongside the most gifted and enlightened among us and one supposes will always prevail, a feature of this may be the born fear of knowledge that is not understood.

In the Garden of Eden version as accepted in ecclesiastical terms, the initial creation where forbidden to approach the tree of knowledge and as such feared it in wonder. It may be that it was at this point, that this negative reluctance or fear of knowledge was first introduced into the human psyche. The initial ET creators would naturally be aware that certain knowledge in the wrong hands can be extremely dangerous. A good example of this would be a psychotic terrorist, yet still intelligent, gaining knowledge of how to construct a so-called dirty bomb by studying the physics and properties of nuclear weapons in order to bring about death and destruction.

Our assumed ET creators would not wish to prevent their initial intelligently enhanced beings from gaining knowledge quite the contrary, after all that is why they were created in the first place. But not until the 'hybrids' where ready and properly assessed with regard to their mental suitability. The alleged serpent in the case of Adam's temptation, would have been (one would imagine) a purposeful test for curiosity, a wish to gain knowledge, signs of obedience, subservience, or defiance, in the subject, in other words a (thorough) review taken of the human psyche, necessary before being released into the world to commence the subduing and populating, however, the wish to gain knowledge was retarded or countered by a remaining fear of ancient wisdom contained in all those ancient scrolls and manuscripts, that was destroyed rather than studied. When we mentioned the possibility that the originally created humans were taken into outer space by the creators, they would have been earmarked as the great human leaders and would be expected to use their knowledge wisely and be taught to write and record all the important factors they were taught, for the sole purpose of learning with regard to their descendants. The outrageous acts of destruction, that took place by fear and human negativity, practically destroyed all the knowledge of the World in a few months. Only snippets remain, that seem too preposterous to believe and in some cases are derived or pass into history as legends, only to be accepted as fables and not to be taken seriously. Of course, with modern day advancement, all that changed. The main factor that would have been taught would of course be their real origins and this would and did pass into legend all over the World and its peoples unto today. This thorough assessment of the various mental qualities in the created 'hybrids' would have been necessary to ensure one of the qualities, that is subservience (obedience) that would be well implanted, so that the 'creators' could select out suitable candidates to be under their control with regard to their future operations on Earth, that is, the historical beings we know as the patriarchs, they must obey without question and have good leadership ability.

By far the best 'hybrid' creation born of a human female would surely have been their specifically created being, we know as Jesus. A quite flawless being, possessed of all the finest qualities that where necessary to convince the masses who still possessed many undesirable traits, that they should follow the righteous path and reject and suppress their negative thoughts and tendencies. The Sermon on the Mount was an example of this unique Rabbi's persuasive teaching and covered all the rewards for humans, if they follow the righteous path. It seems strange today that there still remains doubt and dissent regarding the existence of the man we know as Jesus. It is quite clearly expressed in the Bible during the appearance of the 'angel' in a blinding light, who was to carry out the implant with regard to Mary who would be the mother of Jesus. It was clearly stated 'Thou shalt conceive in the womb and bring forth a son and shalt call his name Jesus'. It couldn't be clearer.

The Bible also contains so much written data on the teachings and miraculous acts carried out by Jesus during his life. Also many of the characters known to have historically existed, such as King Herod, Pontius Pilate and others, tend to reinforce the existence of Jesus.

However, the same human negativity and fear displayed itself in the suspicion and reluctance to believe or consider possible, the many things conveyed to the masses by this unique Rabbi, who many believe, was the long awaited 'Messiah'. Of course others preceded Jesus who some believed was the Messiah, one example of such, was John the Baptist, although he did make it clear that "One will come after me, who will be greater than I".

Clearly the people where forewarned with regard to the forthcoming appearance of the 'true' Messiah, yet still supported his crucifixion, displaying yet again the undesirable qualities in the human.

John the Baptist of course met his end by being beheaded through fear of his teachings.

PILLARS OF FIRE

These undesirable qualities still exist of course in the human psyche. Soapbox characters in Hyde Park for example, 'preacher of our time' and of course, religious groups who gather in most cities singing religious songs, with a small band of musicians etc., and hand out leaflets to all who pass, have to experience also, in the crowd, a handful of rude and disrespectful people who are happy to jeer and make negative comments, rather like the crowd shouting 'crucify him'. There is a school of thought that considers that Apollonius of Tyana could have been the teacher known as Jesus. Apollonius was a philosopher and teacher travelled not only in Mesopotamia but much further. Apollonius was born around 4 BC and would fit the time period of Jesus. During his travels he approached the frontier of Babylon. The guard approached and asked Apollonius "What gifts have you brought for the King?" "All the virtues" replied Apollonius. The guard replied "Do you suppose our King does not already have them". The traveller replied "He may have them but does he know how to use them".

The guard was intrigued by this bold reply and instead of refusing him to pass had the idea that the King himself may be interested in meeting this bold adventurer.

There is another interesting event or parallel in the comparison to Jesus and his early life where it is written that he was too wise to be taught. At the age of fourteen, his school teachers could no longer instruct him because of his inborn intelligence.

Apollonius had great wisdom and could also cure the sick. Knowledge of this had spread to such an extent, that there was a frequently used saying that appeared in Cappadocia "What's the hurry rushing to see young Apollonius?" The teacher and healer travelled to the east; in Mespila (Nineveh) he took the services of a guide called Damis. They travelled far to the east, Apollonius made a strange statement "Learned men were living on the Earth and at the same time not on it".

He received a mission from the adepts of Asia; he "Was to shake the tyranny of Rome". He arrived in Rome at the unfavourable period of the persecutions sanctioned by the Roman Emperor.

When his presence became known, he was summoned to a tribunal. As the Prosecutor unrolled the scroll with the listed charges against him, uncannily the page turned blank and the Court had no option but to release him, without any charges against him, they could do no other.

However, the Roman Authorities still had a superstitious fear of this wise man from Tyana (once again highlighting this inborn negative attitude in the human psyche). It was said that he fared better under Vespasian; also, the

PILLARS OF FIRE

Emperor Titus said to him "I have indeed taken Jerusalem but you Apollonius have captured me".

Strangely, history does not mention the date of this wise sage's death. During his stay in Asia, it is said that he studied at the fee of 'those who knew everything'.

Eventually the memory of Apollonius became so respected that Septimus Severus who ruled the Roman Empire from 193 to 211 for our era had a statue of this memorable being erected in his shrine, together with those of Jesus Christ and Orpheus. Clearly, over the centuries the positive teachings in a Christian orientated fashion where gradually having a positive effect on the greatest pagan empire of the time and carried on doing so up to that time of Emperor Constantine.

All the above data regarding the great sage Apollonius was taken from the life story recorded by Philostratus by request of the Byzantine Empress Domna.

The many comparisons to Jesus and his life are obvious but there are many factors that refute it. Jesus restricted his travels, teachings and cures largely between Nazareth, Galilee and Jerusalem, where Apollonius even travelled to Tibet. The fact is that Apollonius was a Greek philosopher born in Tyana.

In Tibet, Apollonius witnessed many strange things. Even on the way there he and his friend and guide Damis, after a difficult trek from Babylon to India, where the two travellers turned north toward the Himalayan Range and Tibet, it was stated that the path by which they had come, disappeared behind them and they seemed to be in a place 'preserved by illusion'.

On the boundary of this wonderland, they were met by a boy who addressed them in Greek and spoke as if he knew they were coming and where expected. Eventually they were presented to the Ruler who Philostratus called 'Iarchus'.

They were shown many scientific marvels that may seem to many when reading of them to be more like science fiction.

Radiant stones turned the night sky into day; they witnessed human 'levitation' (remembering that Solomon demonstrated this in the presence of the Queen of Sheba).

They also witnessed automations that served food and drink to the weary travellers, these robots were said to be "obedient to the beck of the gods".

Iarchus stated to Apollonius "You have come to men who know everything", he also stated that "The universe is a living thing".

PILLARS OF FIRE

In comparison to Jesus, whose death by crucifixion is well documented in the scriptures. It seems strange that the death of Apollonius was not so recorded, he simply faded away.

With regard to the suggestion that the amazing things witnessed by Apollonius where more like science fiction, we should more accurately say, that if such things where demonstrated to the ancients they would take that view, but with respect to our modern day technology, they can all be (except possibly for levitation) duplicated by our science today.

With all these sages teachers and philosophers and futuristic events being demonstrated, our hypothetical 'angels' or creators must have been quite satisfied with the achievements of their forbears from the time of their great 'creation' programme in Eden.

Tibet has always been a place of great wonderment and intrigue and many other travellers have written regarding its mysteries that many regard as 'tall tales'. It is entirely possible that the more enlightened subjects of the 'human creation where transported there perhaps for their own safety. Clearly, with the same old negative forces that still prevail in the human psyche, they would be feared of being attacked and destroyed. We could mention the comparison of the huge time span between the time of the Caliph Omar and his statement regarding the ancient scrolls, "If they are in our sacred book we know of them already. If not they are foreign and dangerous to us", yet this was still happening in Nazi Germany with the burning of the masses of books on philosophy and esoteric subjects feared by that regime. It must be clear that the greatest challenge to the angelic 'creators' would be an urgent need to rid humanity of these retarding factors and this brings us back to the alleged nurturing and development of all those foetuses mentioned in hypnotic regression tests on those females who proclaim they were abducted and what they had witnessed in the alien craft giving more weight to the theory that they are being gradually inserted into human life minus these retarding qualities (or just as likely to the ETs home planet). If alleged ETs can remove the foetus from the womb in the case of phantom pregnancies they must have the ability to deeply subdue the subject so, equally they could insert an un-bred foetus in the same manner. It is a fact that many a child displays real aspects of high 'intelligence', even before infant school, there have been many child geniuses past and present. It must have been a very delicate 'balancing act' carried out by our supposed ET creators, when blending advanced genetic material with pre-human DNA and occasionally some kind of chemical reaction in the brain, has caused beings (such as I have mentioned in another of my manuscripts) to be born with amazingly intelligent mental ability coupled with retardation in other areas of the brain controlling our behaviour patterns. I would mention the case of two people ignobly referred to as idiot/geniuses. Their names where

Charles and George. Although the word 'idiot geniuses' seems a contradiction in the terms, it appears to classify them adequately. They had been inmates of a California Institute since the age of nine. Yet they displayed one narrow field, sheer mathematical genius. They knew instantly when any given date, centuries ahead, fell on a Sunday. They could also do this in regard to past dates. They would tell you the birth date of any notable being from history and how old they would be if alive today.

Amazingly they could recall any day in their own lives and state whether it was cloudy, rainy or sunny and never miss, yet for all this, they were incapable of completing even the most basic sums of addition, subtraction or division.

Naturally, they were studied closely in an attempt to diagnose their capabilities but when probed as how they were capable of doing it they gave a lopsided drooling grin and said, "it's all in my head".

It would seem that the unused areas of the brain in its over-endowed volume seemed to be occurring in their case but not in a uniformed manner.

Text books on psychology have stated "Arithmetical prodigies have been found among the ranks of the feeble minded".

We mentioned that the brain of Einstein has been preserved, analysed and studied and one wonders if the brain of the aforementioned Charles and George where preserved and analysed regarding the way in which they were wired. If not, they certainly should have been, because even if classified as 'idiot geniuses' in one respect they far exceed the mental qualities of Einstein. All this surely indicates the primary aim of our ET creators was to eventually have all of their human hybrids using all the areas of the brain, actively operating on a par with the areas displayed in the brains of Charles and George.

Perhaps this is the reason the human brain has been bestowed with all this currently unused cellular material and in the future we will be the 'gods' or at least equal to them. We may have mentioned a certain Dr. Robert Plomin and his team, who after a six year search isolated a gene that governs intelligence; this is really quite startling to discover a gene that may have been inserted by our ET creators would be like finding alien artifacts on the Earth. The programme that discovered this was called 'Equinox' and shown on Channel 4 in 1997. We have to imagine, if we can, discover a gene that governs intelligence, why can we not discover genes that retard the brains of the aforementioned Charles and George or those that are responsible for all the negative aspects of the human behaviour patterns. If so, we would then be closer to the production of a super human in terms of mental ability who may, by the use of such an organ, discover the identity of those who began that process of hastening the brains development that began so long ago in their mysterious Garden of Eden. We have come a long way since the Dominican monk Giordano Bruno who was burnt alive at the Piazza De-Fiore in Rome as a heretic but we still have a long way to go. However, the process seems to be accelerating. Almost every day astronomers and astrologists discover things that astound them and will occupy their time for quite a lengthy period to come. Even moon rocks retrieved by Apollo Eleven fifty years ago still have unanswered questions with regard to their makeup; One moon rock was described as like a piece of marble cake, made up of different pieces not all of the same age or composition. If there are no unforeseen interruptions of scientific and technological advancement, such as those in the dark ages, an interesting future looks to be certain for humanity.

Of course, it was religious pressure and a refusal to believe the discoveries of 'satanic science', that severely punished those responsible. It is strange to relate, that scholars and clerics of comparatively recent times thought that the Earth was but a few thousand years old yet ancient Brahim books estimated the 'day of Brahma' that the life span of our solar system to be four billion three hundred and twenty years. This figure is very close to our currently estimated age of four billion six hundred years. Thankfully science has emerged from medieval darkness today, but the darkness should not have existed, there where amazingly accurate statements made in the past, so accurate today. If such ideas and knowledge had been allowed to steadily progress, our present day technology would be seriously advanced.

Consider the following, Pythagoras (6th century BC) taught at his school in Crotona, that the Earth was a sphere, Aristarchus of Samos deduced the Earth revolved around the sun.

As an example of the very advanced knowledge written and lodged in the great repositories the circumference of the earth was computed by Eratosthenes the Librarian of Alexandria. This gives us a good idea of the quality of the information, much of which would have been pillaged during the aforesaid destructions.

The kind of knowledgeable data that the unfortunate Giordano Bruno paid for with his life was profoundly accurate. In one of his books he stated that there are an infinite number of suns in the universe and that there are planets that revolve around them. Some of these worlds might be populated, he said.

How could the ancients know or have come by all this accurate data? In Bruno's time it was well after the destructive rampages, it does not appear logical to assume he guessed it. So he was either verbally informed or had access to some data that was saved from destruction.

Ancient Greek philosophers believe in the plurality of worlds, two thousand years before Bruno. They informed Alexander the Great that although he had conquered most of the world, there were many others in infinite space.

Anaxagoras also wrote about other Earths in the universe. We may dwell on the fact that the Greek philosophers and enlighteners followed the ancient Egyptians. Remembering that their scribes and priests spoke of the precession of the equinoxes in a roundabout way by stating that the sun did not always rise at the point we know today. Knowledge going back into the dim dark past of twenty six thousand years is quite mind boggling as that is as long as it takes for the polar axis to rotate through the zodiac. Perhaps this explains the aforementioned event when Apollonius in Tibet stood at the feet of those how know everything.

With regard to mathematics and extremely high numbers, until Descartes and Leibniz, the Europeans had no concept of the million but the ancient Hindus and Babylonians and Egyptians had hieroglyphics for one million and manipulated astronomical figures in their records. The Egyptian symbol for one million was a man looking amazed with both hands in the air.

In ancient India the digit 'zero' was used long before our era. As for civil structures and town planning, around 2,500 BC, the cities of Mohenjo Daro and Harappa, in what is now Pakistan they were as carefully planned as Paris or Washington. They had efficient water supply, drainage and rubbish chutes where provided.

Clearly there was a golden age long before our era. Why did all these advancements decline and disappear? One can understand written knowledge disappearing without trace but not such early advancements and techniques, the ability to carry on with them must have been in the minds of the constructors and apprentices, those that descended from the original builders in order to carry on with this work elsewhere and preserve the skills and techniques. Consider another example of this degeneration in all quarters, in late 1500s Europeans did not use (or have) spoons and forks; they used only knives and fingers. The ancient Egyptians used spoons as early as 3,000 BC.

The Alexandrian Library was also a University and Research Institute. It had faculties of medicine, mathematics, astronomy, literature and many other subjects. It also had a chemical lab and astronomical theatre and an anatomical unit for operations and dissections; it even had a botanical and zoological garden. What a wonderful place it must have been. Small wonder scholars from all over the world travelled to study in and admire it.

One can only imagine how the history of science would have developed over the millennia to our time. If it had remained intact. As for today, we can only depend on disconnected fragments, casual passages and meagre scraps of knowledge. However, we must remember that (it is said) many documents and data still remain undeciphered. Of course, it is still possible to discover lost knowledge by accident or excavation in those areas. A good example of which occurred about 1820 when the French Egyptologist Champollion visited the Turin Museum. In a box he went through in the store room containing pieces of Papyri. He was told it was only useless rubbish but when Champollion put the pieces together, it turned out to be the only extant list of Egyptian Dynasties, with the names of the Pharoes and the dates of their reigns.

Clearly a more accurate view of the world's past history will emerge if we continually find such treasures. We could refer to the Dead Sea scrolls.

The same prevailing ignorance and fear of knowledge still existed with regard to the unrecognised writings of the Maya during the rampages of the conquistadors, Diego de Landa (described as an overzealous monk) discovered a large library of Maya codices in Mexico. He stated, "We burnt them all because they contained nothing but superstition and Machinations of the devil". Does this not mirror the remarks of the Caliph Omar we previously mentioned? How could he make such a statement when he couldn't read them to judge?

The descendants of our assumed ET creators must have been, over the millennia, continually delighted then frustrated after all the hard work of their predecessors to nurture intelligence in the developing human.

Diego De Landa when older was quite ashamed of his actions. He had become a Bishop. He searched for other Mayan scripts but with no success. This account is from *We are not the first*, by Andrew Tomas (Sphere). He stated that three miraculously surviving manuscripts of the Maya still remain undeciphered today.

This may not be the case now; because when he made that statement in his book it was some decades ago. Another unexpected discovery was the manuscript depicting the history of the Incas. It had lain in obscurity for centuries but it turned up in The Royal Library of Copenhagen in 1908, it was finally published in 1927.

We mentioned when dealing with the life of Abraham that he came from Ur in Mesopotamia, but it wasn't clear where it was situated and was not afforded any historical significance or geographical location, until Sir Leonard Woolly discovered it in his excavations. Of course, the same suspicion applied to the references regarding the city of Troy in the *Iliad* or *Odyssey* of Homer. However, Heinrich Schliemann had faith in its true existence and discovered the ancient city, having read the *Iliad*; he even discovered the cup that was decorated with doves which was said Odysseus used, he found the 3,600 year old cup in a deep mineshaft.

Folklore often portrays actual history in disguise. Fortunately, some historians take it seriously and are often rewarded for their efforts. The history of the Minoans was looked on with suspicion and it is said, that the Greeks themselves knew nothing about their predecessors, the Minoans.

In 1952, Michael Ventris decoded the Linear B script of Crete which he found was early Greek. Plato in his dialogues had mentioned it when discussing the birthplace of Zeus in Crete. But his contemporaries had never heard of pre-classical Greek. However, when an ancient script was found in the late nineteenth century it turned out to be pre-classic Greek.

Today perhaps we could take Plato's account of the once existing lost island of Atlantis more seriously. People where amused when Parmenides, in the 6th century, stated that the moon illuminates the night sky by 'borrowed' light which of course is correct, light borrowed from the sun.

When we spoke of many references to what appear to be archaic structures on the moon, an ancient Brahmin tradition teaches that 'Lunar Pitris (patriarchs) created all life on this planet after descending from the moon'.

This is interesting and could be related to our assumption that our suspected advanced ET creators when first arriving in our solar system established themselves firstly on the moon to assess its value for rare minerals and to formulate their plans for their earthly operations and eventually begin their great creational programme to enhance and further the spread of intelligence and creativity which we feel may be the reason that we exist today.

The aforementioned Sanskrit texts made it clear that there was an awareness that the moon is an ancient body, and stood for the 'cradle of life'. In Mayan art, the moon is depicted as an old man. We are certainly aware today due to the retrieval of so many moon rocks that the moon is ancient, even indicating it could be older than the Earth itself when dating some of the moon rocks. We know that the moon affects the tides on Earth. But how did Seleucus an ancient astronomer of Babylon know it? He explained that the tides of the seas are affected by lunar attraction. Even Julius Caesar wrote that when the moon is full the tides are high and waited for the high spring tides to land in England.

We mentioned that since our hypothetical descendants of the original ET creators still remain on Earth and manifest their presence in the UFO phenomena. Their great memory banks would surely have recorded all of human advancement and also their decline, during the Dark Ages. However, one would imagine that apart from the spectre of negative and destructive actions, that still hover over human advancements, they would be largely satisfied that their predecessors had achieved a great success with the additional brain material they provided which should ultimately eliminate through advancement all the brains' undesirable qualities. 'Conclusion', mission successful, before and after, their descending on their 'Pillars of Fire'.

REFERENCES

CHAPTER I

1. Holy Bible old Testament Book of Samuel 7 Chapter 12
2. Holy Bible – Luke 1

CHAPTER II

1.	Genesis Book 1 Chapter 1 Para. 2	Holy Bible	British and Foreign Bible Society	1957
2.	Genesis Book 1 Chapter 1 Para. 12	Holy Bible	British and Foreign Bible Society	1957
3.	Genesis Book Chapter 1 Para. 20	Holy Bible	British and Foreign Bible Society	1957
4.	Genesis Book Chapter 1 Para 26	Holy Bible	British and Foreign Bible Society	1957
5.	Genesis Book 1 Chapter 1 Para 26	Holy Bible	British and Foreign Bible Society	1957
6.	Genesis Book Chapter 1 Para. 30	Holy Bible	British and Foreign Bible Society	1957
7.	Genesis Book 1 Chapter 2 Paras. 10-14	Holy Bible	British and Foreign Bible Society	1957
8.	The Bible Alive Page (and plate) 63		Harper Collins	1993
9.	Genesis Book Chapter 2 Para. 8	Holy Bible	British and Foreign Bible Society	1957
10.	Genesis Book 1 Chapter 2 Para. 28	Holy Bible	British and Foreign Bible Society	1957
11.	Genesis Book 1 Chapter 2 Para. 19	Holy Bible	British and Foreign Bible Society	1957

12.	Genesis Book Chapter 2 Para. 21	Holy Bible	British and Foreign Bible Society	1957
13.	Genesis Book Chapter 3 Para. 22	Holy Bible	British and Foreign Bible Society	1957
13a.	Lost Worlds	Robert Charroux	Fontana	1974
14.	Genesis Book Chapter 3 Para. 29	Holy Bible	British and Foreign Bible Society	1957
15.	Genesis Book Chapter 4 Para. 17	Holy Bible	British and Foreign Bible Society	1957
16.	Genesis Book 1 Chapter 4 Para. 16	Holy Bible	British and Foreign Bible Society	1957
17.	Secrets of the Lost Races Page 29	Rene Noorbergen	Nel paperback	1980
18.	Genesis Book Chapter 5 Para. 32	Holy Bible	British and Foreign Bible Society	1957
19.	Genesis Book 1 Chapter 6 Paras. 2 & 4	Holy Bible	British and Foreign Bible Society	1957
20.	Genesis Book 1 Chapter 6 Para. 7	Holy Bible	British and Foreign Bible Society	1957
21.	Genesis Book 1 Chapter 6 Para. 9	Holy Bible	British and Foreign Bible Society	1957
22.	Genesis Book 1 Chapter 6 Para. 14	Holy Bible	British and Foreign Bible Society	1957
23.	Genesis Book 1 Chapter 7 Para. 16	Holy Bible	British and Foreign Bible Society	1957
24.	Genesis Book 1 Chapter 7 Para. 24	Holy Bible	British and Foreign Bible	1957

25. Genesis Book 1 Chapter 9 Para. 3	Holy Bible	Society British and Foreign Bible Society	1957
26. Genesis Book 1 Chapter 8 Para. 1	Holy Bible	British and Foreign Bible Society	1957
27. Genesis Book 1 Chapter 6 Para. 15	Holy Bible	British and Foreign Bible Society	1957
28. Secrets of the Lost Races Page 42	Rene Noorbergen	Nel Paperback	1980
29. Genesis Book 1 Chapter 11 Para 1	Holy Bible	British and Foreign Bible Society	1957
30. Genesis Book 1 Chapter 11 Para. 5	Holy Bible	British and Foreign Bible Society	1957
31. Genesis Book 1 Chapter 11 Para. 6	Holy Bible	British and Foreign Bible Society	1957
32. Genesis book 1 Chapter 11 Para. 7	Holy Bible	British and Foreign Bible Society	1957

CHAPTER III

1. GENESIS 12: 1 – 3
2. GENESIS 28: 10 – 22
3. GENESIS 13: 14 – 15
4. GENESIS 18:
5. GENESIS   8 – 25
6. GENESIS 19: 7 – 8
7. GENESIS 19: 33

CHAPTER IV

1. EXODUS   1:   2 – 9
2. EXODUS   2:   10
3. EXODUS   2:   11 – 22
4. EXODUS   3 – 6

5. EXODUS   7 – 10
6. EXODUS   11:1 12 – 50
7. EXODUS   11 – 13
8. EXODUS   14:   15
9. EXODUS   16 – 17
10. EXODUS   20
11. EXODUS   32
12. EXODUS 25:1, 31:11, 35:30, 40:38

CHAPTER V

1. JOSHUA   1: 16 – 17
2. JOSHUA   3 – 5
3. JOSHUA   6
4. JOSHUA   13 – 22
5. JOSHUA   23 – 24

CHAPTER VI

1.	Judges Chapter 13. Paras. 18 & 20	Holy Bible	British and Foreign Bible Society	1957
2.	Lost Worlds Page 183	Robert Charroux	Fontana/ Collins	1975
3.	Samuel Chapter 5 Paras. 19 & 24	Holy Bible	British and Foreign Bible Society	1957
4.	Samuel Chapter 6 Paras. 6 & 7	Holy Bible	British and Foreign Bible Society	1957
5.	Samuel Chapter 7 Para. 12	Holy Bible	British and Foreign Bible Society	1957
6.	Samuel Chapter 22 Para. 20	Holy Bible	British and Foreign Bible Society	1957
7.	Samuel Chapter 22 Paras. 8, 10, 11	Holy Bible	British and Foreign Bible Society	1957
8.	Kings Chapter 8 Para. 10	Holy Bible	British and Foreign Bible Society	1957

PILLARS OF FIRE

9.	Kings Chapter 8 Paras. 8 & 9	Holy Bible	British and Foreign Bible Society	1957
10.	Kings Chapter 8 Para. 27	Holy Bible	British and Foreign Bible Society	1957
11.	Kings Chapter 10 Para. 7	Holy Bible	British and Foreign Bible Society	1957
12.	Kings Chapter 10 Para. 5	Holy Bible	British and Foreign Bible Society	1957
13.	Kings Chapter 18 Para 44	Holy Bible	British and Foreign Bible Society	1957
14.	Kings Chapter 19 Para. 11	Holy Bible	British and Foreign Bible Society	1957
15.	Kings Book 2 Chapter 2 Para 8	Holy Bible	British and Foreign Bible Society	1957
16.	Kings Book 2 Chapter 2 Para. 11	Holy Bible	British and Foreign Bible Society	1957
17.	Kings Book 2 Chapter 5 Para. 32	Holy Bible	British and Foreign Bible Society	1957
18.	Ezekiel Chapter 4 Para. 15	Holy Bible	British and Foreign Bible Society	1957
19.	Ezekiel Chapter 10 Para 19	Holy Bible	British and Foreign Bible Society	1957
20.	Ezekiel Chapter 11 Para 1	Holy Bible	British and Foreign Bible Society	1957
21.	Daniel Chapter 6 Para. 22	Holy Bible	British and Foreign Bible Society	1957
22.	Matthew Chapter 9 Para. 27	Holy Bible	British and Foreign Bible	1957

PILLARS OF FIRE

23. Matthew Chapter 13 Para. 47	Holy Bible	British and Foreign Bible Society	1957
24. Matthew Chapter 28 Para. 2	Holy Bible	British and Foreign Bible Society	1957
25. Acts of the Apostles Chapter 1 Para 9-11	Holy Bible	British and Foreign Bible Society	1957

CHAPTER VII AND CONCLUSION

1. Secrets of the Lost Races	Rene Noorbergen	Nel Paperbacks	1980
2. The Interrupted Journey	John Fuller	Corgi	1981
3. Gods and Spacemen in the Ancient East (5th tablet, The Epic of Gilgamesh)	W. Raymond Drake	Sphere	1976
4. Gods and Spacemen in the Ancient East (5th tablet, The Epic of Gilgamesh)	W. Raymond	Sphere	1976
5. Atlantis and the Giants	D. Saurat	Faber and Faber London	1972
6. We are not the First	Andrew Tomas	Sphere	1972
7. Jesus Christ Heir to the Astronauts	Gerhard Steinhauser	Coronet	1976
8. The Babylonian Story of the Flood	W.G. Lambert	Oxford	1969
9. Jesus Christ Heir to the Astronauts	Gerhard Steinhauser	Coronet	1976
10. Jesus Christ Heir to the Astronauts	Gerhard Steinhauser	Coronet	1976
11. The Holy Bible	ECC. 1: 9-10	British and Foreign Bible Society	1957
12. We are not the First	Andrew Tomas	Sphere	1972
13. We are not the First	Andrew Tomas	Sphere	1972
14. Someone Else is on our Moon	George H. Leonard	Sphere	1977

****

www.ingramcontent.com/pod-product-compliance
Lightning Source LLC
Chambersburg PA
CBHW020804160426
43192CB00006B/431